CROSS AND PEER TUTORING:

HELP FOR CHILDREN WITH LEARNING PROBLEMS

Joseph R. Jenkins
Linda M. Jenkins

What Research and Experience Say to the Teacher of Exceptional Children

The Council for Exceptional Children

Published in 1981 by The Council for Exceptional Children, 1920 Association Drive, Reston, Virginia 22091

A product of the ERIC Clearinghouse on Handicapped and Gifted Children.

Library of Congress Number 80-68283

ISBN 0-86586-110-2

This publication was prepared with funding from the National Institute of Education. US Department of Education under contract no. 400-76-0119. Contractors undertaking such projects under government sponsorship are encouraged to express freely their judgment in professional and technical matters. Prior to publication the manuscript was submitted to The Council for Exceptional Children for critical review and determination of professional competence. This publication has met such standards. Points of view, however, do not necessarily represent the official view or opinions of either The Council for Exceptional Children, National Institute of Education, or Department of Education.

Printed in the United States of America.

Contents

What Research and Experience Say to the Teacher of Exceptional Children

Series Editor: June B. Jordan

Series Editorial Committee: Carolyn M. Callahan, Herbert T. Goldstein, Alice H. Hayden, Merle B. Karnes, Thomas C. Lovitt, Joseph S. Renzulli

Other published titles in the Series:

About the Authors

Joseph R. Jenkins is the Director of the Experimental Education Unit, Child Development and Mental Retardation Center, and Professor of Special Education, at the University of Washington in Seattle. His research interests include assessment of and program development for mildly handicapped youngsters, basic reading skills and comprehension, applied behavior analysis, and data based instruction.

Linda M. Jenkins received her Master's in Special Education from the University of Delaware. She has been a public school teacher for 13 years. Currently, Ms. Jenkins is employed as a special education resource room teacher in the Lake Washington School District, Kirkland, Washington. She has implemented a tutoring program in five different sites and has done research in reading, tutoring, and data based instruction.

Preface

This little book about tutoring was undertaken at the request of CEC and the urging of some of our university and public school colleagues. In contemplating this venture, we rejected a strong temptation to write a cookbook detailing how to install and manage a tutoring program in the schools. Rather, we set out to construct a rationale for tutoring as a serious intervention for aiding low performing youngsters and to distill the scientific knowledge extracted from the research on this topic. Based on this research evidence and on several years of personal experience with real life tutoring programs we have addressed some concerns and some questions that practitioners encounter when they contemplate establishing tutoring programs, and have attempted to provide information that will help them with decisions related to these questions.

As usual, the scientific knowledge base for this topic is rather incomplete even though many investigators have studied various aspects of tutoring. However, at the risk of preempting our own findings, we can say that while a number of important issues remain unresolved, there is fairly convincing evidence that the addition of tutoring to the regular school program can have quite significant, beneficial effects on children's achievement.

Credit for the empirically derived knowledge on tutoring goes to hundreds of researchers. Credit for our personal knowledge on the topic is due largely to Bill Mayhall's and Linda Jenkins' work in designing cross age tutoring programs for handicapped and economically disadvantaged youngsters who were failing to learn basic academic skills. Linda Jenkins, for example, has conducted tutoring programs in Delaware, New Mexico, Illinois, and Washington State, some in the context of special education, others within Title I programs. Of course, the real credit for our personal knowledge must be shared with the many children who participated as tutors and learners, the cooperating teachers who restructured their classroom schedules to accommodate the tutoring programs, the school principals who supported and encouraged these programs, and the special education graduate students who received practicum training in connection with public school resource rooms where tutoring was conducted and who themselves contributed ideas for upgrading the quality of the programs. A number of anecdotes are described in the ensuing material. In those cases where we have used tutored children's names, we have substituted other names in the interest of confidentiality.

The authors are grateful to Constance Pious for her comments and editorial help on an earlier version of this manuscript.

Prologue

This monograph focuses on tutoring as a means of improving student achievement. The rationale that we develop for establishing tutoring programs is based on the need to improve the achievement levels of handicapped and disadvantaged students. It may appear that we view academic achievement as an end in itself and as the only problem area in which these students need attention. Nothing could be further from the truth. Many handicapped and disadvantaged children lack appropriate interpersonal skills related to establishing and maintaining friendships, handling conflicts, and matching behaviors to different situations. These skills must be learned if students are to avoid disqualification from the educational mainstream.

Equally important, however, is acquisition of academic skills. Most referrals to special education result from retarded academic development, particularly in the area of reading. Reflecting on the goals and purposes of schooling, Stoddard (1961) and Reynolds and Birch (1978) have refered to reading, writing, and arithmetic as the cultural imperatives, capabilities which schools have been created to instill in maturing youth. Society sees the cultural imperatives as the central concern of the educational establishment and charges it with meeting these imperatives.

Serious consequences emanate from a failure to achieve commensurate with the standards set by society, and these consequences have far reaching effects both on the person and society itself. Some are progressive, as when daily exposures to failure and defeat propel young persons down an emotional path leading from anxiety to discouragement to apathy to alienation. Some consequences are abrupt, as when students are disqualified from regular education to be reassigned to programs that separate them from regular classmates and from the social as well as learning opportunities that characterize normalized educational environments. Other consequences of unsatisfactory achievement are delayed, but equally negative, ranging from restricted career and vocational opportunities to reduced recreational and material advantages. Thus, we justify our concern with the cultural imperatives of academic achievement not because they are the only problem confronting handicapped children and their teachers, but because they are a primary goal of schooling and are capable of producing a profound and permanent influence on a person's life.

1 The Rationale for Tutoring

Children with learning disabilities, mental retardation, behavior disorders, and sensory handicaps have one characteristic in common. They acquire basic academic and social skills at a slower rate than do their nonhandicapped peers. In this respect they are similar to many children who are raised in impoverished environments or whose native language is other than English. To the extent that these children fail to master basic academic and social skills which society holds to be essential, they have been and will remain cut off from many benefits enjoyed by their normally achieving peers.

CHALLENGE TO TEACHERS

The task facing professionals who teach these children is clear enough—how to raise achievement rates and thereby reduce the discrepancy between handicapped children and their peers. It is less clear just how this task can be accomplished, particularly when one examines the rather dismal record of previous attempts to help children with learning problems. Evaluations of special education programs have, more often than not, found that handicapped children achieve no better as a result of placement in special programs. For the most part, evaluations of remedial services for regular education students have not yielded any better news; the effect of Title I programs and remedial reading programs are often too small to detect. Later in this chapter we will propose some reasons why these programs may have failed.

At any rate, teachers face a hefty challenge in arranging humane yet effective conditions that will maximize cognitive and emotional

1

growth for handicapped children. By itself, teaching is not that difficult. Teachers with whom we have talked are confident that they could teach almost anything to nearly anyone, if they had the time. The fact that Maxine requires 80 repetitions of a rule before she can apply it consistently is a problem only if her teacher has insufficient time to provide the repetitions. Of course, time spent with Maxine is probably time taken away from other students who have already learned Maxine's rule or who are at an earlier spot in the curriculum. Whether or not, or when, Maxine learns the rule will probably not be determined by her teacher's ability to teach, but by her teacher's available time. The problem faced by Maxine's teacher—that of getting sufficient time for teaching Maxine—is a function of class size and of the varieties of human differences found in schools.

ACCOMMODATING INDIVIDUAL DIFFERENCES

Two types of human differences contribute to the teacher's problem in providing adequate instructional time. One is the difference in what children already know. Some children need to be taught to count and to read. Others arrive at school with these skills intact. Some need to be taught how to draw cause and effect inferences; others are already quite capable in this regard. Some need to be taught the meaning of the words *left, right, under, damage, bulge,* and *irritated.* Others have learned these meanings already. Differences in previously acquired knowledge complicate the teacher's world because they mean that different children will require instructional time on different learning tasks.

The second type of difference among children that complicates the job of teaching was already illustrated in the case of Maxine. Children require different amounts of instruction to master the same skill. If a teacher has four children who need to learn the sounds for /a/, /m/, /t/, and /s/, she can form a small group and provide daily instruction on these elements. A problem arises when one student learns the sounds after one day, the second student after three days, the third after five, and the last finally masters the sounds after eight days. Such situations are commonplace, and there are almost no completely satisfactory resolutions for these problems in different learning rates. One solution, keeping all students on the same task until everyone has learned, will impede the faster students' progress. Alternatively, abandoning the task before all students have mastered it will almost certainly guarantee subsequent failure for the slow students. Breaking up the larger group into two smaller groups is a partial solution, but even then remaining differences in learning rate will prevent some students from making optimum progress. A second difficulty with this latter solution is that it reduces available instructional time. To illustrate, if 20 minutes were originally scheduled for instructing a group of four students, then dividing this group into two reduces instructional time for each group to 10 minutes. Thus, attempts to provide for individual differences often result in a reduction of instructional time for any single student.

Without a satisfactory solution to this problem, efforts to individualize instruction usually take the form of private seatwork, as evidenced by the proliferation of student workbooks. We believe that the ability of workbooks to teach useful skills has been vastly overrated. More often than not, their major value is to occupy a portion of the class so that a teacher can instruct a small group without interruption. Unfortunately, the distinction between teaching and keeping children occupied has grown blurred, so that some individuals have come to believe that children learn reading skills by completing workbook pages.

The absurdity of this position is apparent when children are kept from moving to the next reading level because they have not or cannot complete the workbooks satisfactorily, even though they are capable of reading and comprehending the reading textbook. Over the years, workbooks have come to dominate classroom instruction. The number of "skills" that workbooks are said to teach has grown geometrically. It is interesting that increases in reading achievement scores have not accompanied the new and "improved" curricula. On the contrary, there is some suggestion that reading achievement scores have declined. We believe that workbooks by themselves cannot be counted upon to individualize reading and math instruction, that their ability to individualize instruction is more apparent than real, and that teachers are faced with an extremely difficult challenge in providing efficient and effective instruction to children who differ both in previously acquired knowledge and learning rate.

LOSS OF INSTRUCTIONAL TIME

Individual differences among students are not the only variables that detract from instructional time. Teachers must collect milk money, take attendance, run dittos, monitor recess, help students who have not brought the right supplies, discipline unruly youngsters, and organize transitions, along with a multitude of other activities that are not directly related to teaching. When this time is subtracted from the school day, the result is a significant reduction in the time available for actual teaching.

The loss of real instructional time, whether resulting from activities extraneous to teaching or from attempts to accommodate for individual differences (as in creating more groups with fewer instructional minutes available for each), would appear, from a common sense analysis, to be a serious matter. Recent research supports this common sense view. Data gathered in elementary classrooms have identified "academic engaged time" as a highly significant correlate of achievement—one that distinguishes classrooms that produce above and below average achievement levels.

What exactly is meant by academic engaged time? The concept, originally developed by Berliner, Fisher, Filby and Marlieve (1976), refers to the time a student spends engaged in academically relevant tasks that are moderately difficult. Academic engaged time is not the same as alloted instructional time. A typical elementary classroom allots from 90 minutes to 2 hours daily to language arts instruction. Observations of what the students do during this period, however, reveal that far fewer minutes are actually spent engaged in a learning task.

Academic engaged time is highly related to content coverage, which itself has been shown to be consistently and significantly related to student achievement gain. In summarizing research on effective classrooms, Rosenshine and Berliner (1978) concluded:

> A fairly consistent pattern emerges from the studies cited. The primary finding is that time spent engaged in relevant content appears to be an essential variable for which there is no substitute.
>
> Teachers who make a difference in students' achievement are those who put students into contact with curriculum materials and find ways to keep them in contact. (p. 12)
>
> Within the area of instruction in basic skills in primary grades, the major skill needed by a teacher is that of obtaining "sufficient" content coverage and academic engaged minutes per day. (p. 13)

A similar theme was struck by researchers who studied effective teachers in programs for handicapped children, classrooms very different from those of Rosenshine and Berliner which were essentially regular education programs. Fredericks, Anderson, Baldwin, Grove, Moore, Moore and Beaird (undated) sought to identify features that distinguished between successful and unsuccessful teachers of severely and moderately handicapped students. Success was defined in terms of student gains over the course of a year. Of 86 indicators studied, the one which accounted for the greatest difference between high and low success groups was the number of minutes of instruction per day. Compared to low achievement teachers, high achievement teachers provided an average of nearly 40 more minutes of instruction daily for their students. Over the school year this amounts to a difference of over 6,700 minutes. To produce these additional minutes of instruction, teachers often used volunteers who taught children individually.

The concepts of academic engaged time and content coverage may help to explain the previously mentioned failures of special and remedial education programs to improve the achievement levels of students with learning problems. Although there is enormous variability among them, special classes for learning disabled and mentally retarded children probably do not, on the average, increase instructional minutes on relevant academic content beyond that available in regular classrooms. Learning disability classrooms are often characterized by a heavy emphasis on perceptual-motor, psycholinguistic, and process oriented activities, none of which appear much related to learning basic skills (Arter & Jenkins, 1979).

Likewise, classrooms for educable mentally retarded students have, at least historically, been notable for their reduced emphasis on academic goals in favor of greater attention to preacademic, social knowledge, crafts, art, and music activities. A study by Stallings and Kaskowitz (1974) is interesting in this connection even though it did not involve handicapped students. Based on observations of 100 first grade and 50 third grade classrooms, these investigations reported consistent, positive correlations between achievement gain and the time spent on reading and mathematics. In contrast, activities involving group time, stories, arts and crafts, active play, toys, puzzles, and academic games *always* yielded negative correlations with achievement.

Remedial programs for disadvantaged children and special education resource room programs for mildly handicapped students, although structured differently from segregated, self contained classrooms for the handicapped, still may suffer from the same failure to increase academic engaged time and content coverage. Children leave their regular classrooms to attend these special programs for some portion of the day. Quite commonly the children's absence from their homerooms coincides with those periods ordinarily devoted to reading and math instruction. Thus, students do not gain potentially valuable minutes of basic skill instruction. Rather, their remedial instruction is merely subtracted from instruction they would receive in the regular programs—resulting in neither a net gain nor a net loss. These special programs might even, in some instances, have unintentional deleterious effects, specifically when they replace academically focused regular classroom time with such nonacademic tasks as perceptual-motor activities, cultural enrichment, esteem building, and discussion or game oriented activities. If current thinking about the importance of academic engaged time is correct, and the foregoing analysis of remedial and special programs is at all valid, then the failure of most special programs to improve achievement should come as no surprise.

INCREASING ACADEMIC ENGAGEMENT

Teacher Led Instruction

There are multiple means available to teachers for increasing students' active engagement in academic tasks. In terms of teacher led instruction, the procedures developed by the Oregon Direct Instruction group

(Becker & Carnine, 1978; Becker & Englemann, 1978) are an extremely effective means of obtaining students' active involvement in learning. The various direct instruction programs (Distar Reading, Language and Arithmetic) are characterized by careful sequencing, teaching to mastery, and systematic review. The fast paced, small group instructional format requires frequent student response, guarantees immediate feedback, and specifies effective procedures for correcting errors. Observation of a Distar group lesson leaves one with no questions about student engagement. Evaluations conducted on the direct instruction programs show them to be unusually effective in producing achievement gain.

The nationwide evaluation of the United States Office of Education Follow-Through programs disclosed that, compared to 22 others, the direct instruction model was consistently the most effective in raising the achievement levels of economically disadvantaged youngsters. The direct instruction results were remarkable not only relative to the other model programs but also in an absolute sense. Children taught in this model scored at or above the 50th percentile of national norms by the end of third grade (Becker, 1977). It is reasonable to assume that Distar's results are due largely to its care in selecting instructional content and to its success in producing student engagement. The Distar small group instruction procedures can be adapted rather easily to other commercial reading programs as well as to other instructional domains. For information on these adaptations one can consult an excellent text by Carnine and Silbert (1979) entitled *Direct Instruction Reading*.

Working Privately

Of course, elementary and secondary students spend only a portion of their time in teacher led instruction. Descriptive studies in elementary classrooms indicate that children, 6 to 11 years old, spend at least half of their school day working privately (Rosenshine & Berliner, 1978). Private, seatwork assignments must be selected with care or it will make no difference that students are task oriented when working by themselves. Assuming that private work assignments are valid, then effective classroom management procedures become important in helping maintain attention and minimizing disruptions or other distractions. Lovitt (1978) has provided an excellent description of classroom and child management procedures available to teachers for insuring high student engagement in seatwork.

One to One Instruction

Since every skill cannot be taught simultaneously, one ordinarily develops a sequence of instructional objectives. Ideally, a student can concentrate on mastering one objective at a time before being presented with the next objective in the sequence. However, as noted earlier, grouping students for instruction usually prevents individuals from making maximum progress. Usually, a child who is instructed in a group will be forced either to proceed onto the next objective before attaining mastery of the current objective or to remain on an objective he or she has already mastered, while waiting for the rest of the class to attain adequate performance.

As long as individual students vary in their learning rates, small group instruction will produce less than optimum rates of progress through an instructional sequence, since by its nature grouping for instruction guarantees that some children will not receive instruction on an objective appropriate for them. Thus, even though a well designed group format can produce high levels of task engagement, the academic engaged time for an individual student (learning relevant content) will be less than the total instructional time for the group. From this analysis, it appears that academic engaged time could be augmented by substituting some one to one instruction for some small group sessions and private seatwork assignments.

Unfortunately, teachers are not themselves capable of providing much individual instruction, as evidenced by the amount of group instruction and private work observed in classrooms. In fact, there is some correlational evidence that teachers who devote much classroom time to individual students are overall less effective, presumably because attention to the individual detracts from the time available for other class members. In the previously cited study by Stallings and Kaskowitz (1974), time spent working with just one or two students was negatively related to achievement gained by the class, but a positive relation was found between achievement gains and time spent working with small or with large groups. Obviously, then, if teachers desire to increase academic engaged time through one to one instruction, they must expand their reserve of instructional personnel. They need not look far. Some of the best helpers are other children who can be recruited from inside their own school. Other resources that are equally effective, although more difficult to tap, are secondary and college students and adult volunteers.

RESEARCH SUPPORT FOR TUTORING

By now, almost every educator has heard the dismaying and counter intuitive news that class size (i.e., teacher-pupil ratio) is not an important factor in how much students learn. Historically, several decades of research on class size was unable to demonstrate a consistent relationship between this variable and student learning. As recently as 1978, Porwell concluded, "There is general consensus that the research findings on the effects of class size on pupil achievement across all grades are contradictory and inconclusive" (Porwell, quoted in Glass & Smith, 1978). Remarkably, the consensus to which Porwell refers happens to be dead wrong. Glass and Smith (1978) recently completed the most comprehensive, statistically sophisticated, and detailed analysis of the class size research ever conducted. Referring to the results of reanalysis of research, they stated, "Indeed, it established clearly that reduced class-size can be expected to produce increased academic achievement" (p. iv).

Why the change? It appears that previous reviewers had made some crucial errors that led them to conclude mistakenly that class size was not important. The most serious of these errors was the inclusion of poorly controlled studies that did not fairly equate pupil ability in the large and small classes, and the failure to discriminate between relative and absolute class size differences. For example, in some studies large-small comparisons were between sizes of 20 and 40, and in others between 100 and 200. In the latter instance, it is not surprising to find little difference in achievement since instruction would probably not differ much in the "large" and "small" classes. When Glass and Smith took into account these factors in their reanalysis of nearly 80 class size studies, which included 900,000 pupils of varying age and ability, they found that the number of well controlled comparisons was substantially reduced, from 700 to only 100. Their conclusions, based on the well controlled studies, are as follows:

As class size increases, achievement decreases. A pupil, who would score at about the 83rd percentile on a national test when taught individually, would score at about the 50th percentile when taught in a class of 40 pupils. The difference in being taught in a class of 20 versus a class of 40 is an advantage of 6 percentile ranks. The major benefits from reduced class size are obtained as size is reduced to 20 pupils.(p. v)

Examination of the curve in Figure 1 reveals that the greatest differences in achievement occur as class sizes approach the lower ratios. That is, differences in achievement are greater with class sizes of 5 versus 10 than with sizes of 10 versus 20.

Corroboration for this phenomenon of increased effects at lower ratios is found in a study by Moody, Bausell, and Jenkins (1973). Normal fourth grade students were taught a half-hour mathematics lesson in class sizes of 1, 2, 5, and 23. On a test especially designed to cover the instructional content, those students taught in smaller groups performed better than those taught in larger groups. Particularly noteworthy was the finding that the greatest drop in learning occurred as class size increased from one (tutoring) to the smallest possible group instruction, a "class" of two. Figure 2 shows the relation of class size to achievement of the math objectives.

Several other studies have contrasted the effects of tutorial and small group instruction. Jenkins, Mayhall, Peschka, and Jenkins (1974) compared teacher led small group instruction with one to one instruction delivered by cross age tutors. The children were learning disabled and mentally retarded youngsters receiving service in special education resource rooms, and the tutors were regular third and fourth

8

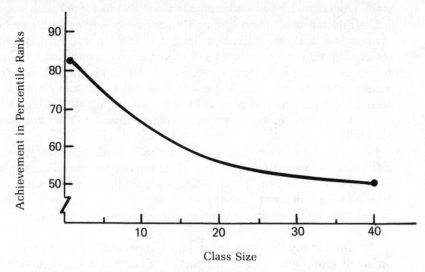

FIGURE 1. Relationship Between Achievement and Class Size. Data Integrated Across Approximately 100 Comparisons from Studies Exercising Good Experimental Control. (From *Meta-analysis of Research on the Relationship of Class-Size and Achievement* by G. V. Glass and M. L. Smith. Laboratory of Educational Research, University of Colorado, 1978. Reprinted by permission.)

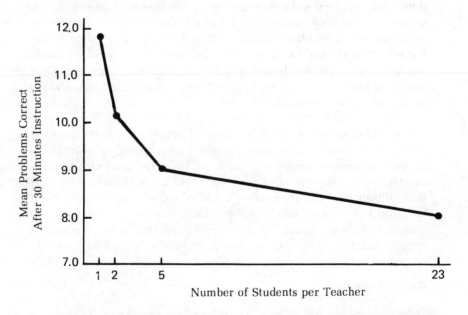

FIGURE 2. Mean Correct Performance under Varying Teacher-Pupil Ratios. (From "The Effects of Class Size on the Learning of Mathematics: A Parametric Study" by W. B. Moody, R. B. Bausell, and J. R. Jenkins, *Journal for Research in Mathematics Education*, 1973, 4, 170-176. Reprinted by permission.)

grade students who had undergone training and had worked as tutors for several months. In this research, each learner served as his or her own control, and was instructed daily in both the teacher led and the tutorial conditions. Learning was observed across several tasks including word recognition, oral reading, spelling, and math facts. The results were entirely consistent with those of Glass and Smith and Moody, et al.: learning was greatest in the tutorial condition, with one to one instruction from a peer exceeding teacher led small group instruction.

In contrast to these findings, two other studies indicated less difference between tutorial and small group instruction (Klosterman, 1970; Shaver & Nuhn, 1971). Both used adults as instructors and relatively unstructured teaching sessions. Although the results were mixed, the small group lessons were sometimes as effective as the tutorials.

One final study deserves mention in connection with the literature on small group and tutorial instruction. Fink and Sandall (undated) used a highly structured small group format, modeled after the Distar programs. Employing a unison response format — i.e., all students responded together to each stimulus presentation—investigators gave moderately retarded preschoolers brief lessons on sight words. The investigators found no difference in the number of words correctly identified by children who underwent this small group treatment and those who received individual tutoring. This finding suggests that requiring unison responding from all group members more nearly approximates the conditions that prevail in a one to one tutoring lesson. Nevertheless, it would still seem that different group members would reach criterion on the lesson content at different times and, thus, would be prevented from making optimum progress through a series of instructional objectives.

Related to this point, Ellson, Harris, and Barber (1968), who studied first grade classrooms for disadvantaged youngsters, found large individual differences in the words taught during the school year. Under regular classroom conditions the ratio between the extremes, i.e., most words taught to least words taught, was 5 to 1. However, for similar children who received tutoring and, thus, who could progress at their individual optimum rates, the ratio was 13 to 1. These data indicate that one consequence of classroom groupings is to substantially reduce individualization in terms of progression through a curriculum sequence.

Cost Efficiency

Program costs are another factor that deserve attention since public education is expensive and grows more expensive every year. Even though the number of children enrolled in schools declines annually and the school budget grows, the real money available to districts has shrunk as a function of mounting inflation reflected in increased costs for salaries, materials, and building maintenance. Moreover, education budgets are further strained by the fact that public schools, especially in urban settings, are faced with educating an increasingly larger portion of high cost, hard to teach children. Proportionately, handicapped and economically disadvantaged children are more highly represented in today's schools than was true in times past.

Diminishing financial reservoirs combined with intensified needs in the schools have placed professionals in a difficult position as they seek to upgrade the quality of public education. They have little choice but to stretch their dollars by prioritizing their needs and seeking more cost effective means of meeting them. One danger in searching out "cost effective" programs is that cost, not effectiveness, becomes the sole criterion for choosing between alternatives. For a program to be cost effective it must first be effective.

A group of special educators in Vermont recently conducted a model cost effectiveness study in which they compared two forms of service delivery to handicapped children, one of which involved cross age tutoring (Armstrong, Conlon, Pierson, & Stahlbrand, 1979). For several years, school districts in Vermont have employed paraprofessional teacher aides to tutor handicapped students. The aides are trained and supervised by special education consulting teachers who design and monitor individualized teaching programs for each special education student. Consulting teachers, in combination with the paraprofessional aides, have proven remarkably effective in assisting handicapped students to remain in the mainstream of regular education (McKenzie, 1972). Like any program, however, this one consumes considerable financial resources, part of which could conceivably be redirected into other special education support services (e.g., communication disorders specialists, physical therapists, occupational therapists and, for that matter, other consulting teachers).

Armstrong and her colleagues, recognizing the need for effective but cost efficient programs, designed an alternative means of service delivery. They recruited and trained high school seniors to work with consulting teachers in tutoring special education students who were failing to master regular education curriculum objectives. Throughout the school year, these high school students tutored three periods a week and conferred with the consulting teacher one additional period weekly. Their students, who came from first through fourth grade classrooms, gained an average of 1.7 months for each month tutored, exactly the same gain registered by equivalent students who were tutored by paraprofessional aides. Armstrong, et al. maintained complete data on the cost associated with training and supervising both the high schoolers and the aides, and the additional cost of salaries for the latter. Results showed that expenses associated with the paraprofessionals were over three times greater than those for the high school tutors, even though both groups were equally effective in facilitating student achievement. The high school students acquired useful teaching, measuring, and managing skills and rated their experience as highly rewarding, stating they would like to participate again and would recommend the program to others. Vermont's findings suggest that cross age tutoring can offer financially pressed public school programs a cost effective means of serving children who might otherwise not receive the services to which they are entitled.

In summary, several lines of research suggest that one to one tutoring has much to offer even when it is conducted by another child. Support for this conclusion comes from the class size literature and comparisons between tutoring and small group instruction. Among the apparent benefits of tutoring are increased academic engaged minutes, more learning within a single lesson, and more optimum progressions through curriculum sequences for the individual learner.

2 Children as Teachers

Even if tutoring has been demonstrated to benefit the children tutored, that clearly is only half of the picture. In programs employing a peer or cross age model where children serve as tutors, it is particularly important to consider the consequences of this experience for the tutors as well as the learners. Obviously, the time that children spend tutoring is time subtracted from some other activity. Depending upon the other activity and its importance to children's growth and enjoyment, tutoring creates the potential for negative effects on the tutor. For example, cross age tutors who miss classroom time that is scheduled for essential teacher led instruction or for private study may suffer academically for the same reasons that children who receive additional instruction from tutors will benefit academically.

A corollary concern is that more able students who serve as tutors are being exploited by someone—the less able students whom they tutor, the teachers who have not done their jobs, or the school administrators who seek easy solutions to staffing problems. Parents, teachers, and principals have occasionally expressed these or similar concerns. Others have taken an entirely opposite view, suggesting that tutoring will help children both in academic, attitudinal, and socialization areas. To shed light on these opposing ideas, researchers have examined both the cognitive and noncognitive effects of having served as a tutor. While the research evidence is less than definitive, it does allow parents and educators to make more intelligent judgments concerning the reality base for the hypothesized positive and negative outcomes of tutoring.

Before turning to that research, a more philosophical, less empirical case might be built for establishing cross age helping relationships in the schools. That is, the value of tutoring may extend beyond the more traditional self centered curriculum goals of achievement and skills acquisition. Coleman (1974), in the report of the Panel on Youth of the President's Science Advisory Committee, proposed that the environment of young people should provide not only an opportunity for acquiring these traditional school goals, but also an opportunity for gaining "social maturity" through assuming responsibilities that affect the

---

CHILDREN'S ATTITUDES TOWARD OTHERS WITH LEARNING PROBLEMS

Tutors Change the Image of the "Special Education" Room

Any negative response about going to the "special education" room quickly disappears after a tutoring program is in operation. Older students are first to notice the change in status. *All* kinds of students go in and out of the resource room; it is no longer necessary to quietly "sneak" into the room. Some of my younger students think that some of the older students who come into the room for special help are tutors. *LMJ, Special Education Resource Teacher*

The most crucial thing that happened when I had tutors was that all the children, smart or slow, wanted to come to the resource room. It seemed to lose any connection with students who had problems. The top kids came as tutors and as teacher helpers, and the low kids came for help. We all worked, made progress academically and socially, and loved every minute of it. We had the school totally confused. *Jan Walker, Special Education Teacher, Oregon, Illinois*

Tutoring Can Change Students' Ideas

One of the challenges of "mainstreaming" is to develop in nonhandicapped youngsters an appropriate sensitivity to peers with handicaps. In this connection, Ms. Nakagawa, who teaches a fourth/fifth grade combination class, reported an interesting class discussion. Four tutors were explaining to their classmates that kids who had trouble learning to read weren't necessarily "dumb." "Sometimes kids try just as hard as us and don't learn. Some children are born with a learning disability. They need special instructions to learn, but they are just as smart as us." Ms. Nakagawa remarked to me that this spontaneous defense given by fifth grader tutors on behalf of children with academic problems reflected a healthy regard for handicapped individuals, and probably did more to foster acceptance than any sermonizing she herself might have done. *LMJ*

---

lives of others. "Only with the experience of such responsibilities can youth move toward the mutually responsible and mutually rewarding involvement with others that constitutes social maturity" (Coleman, quoted in Allen, 1976).

Society holds to an ideal that children will grow into responsible citizens who care for and help others. Yet inexplicably, within its major institution for socializing the young, the school, it rarely permits children to assume and practice these responsibilities. Nor does it systematically supervise or actively shape effective helping behaviors. Thus, were education to seriously accept as one of its goals the development of social maturity, it might include more opportunities and experiences that would facilitate attainment of this goal.

However, the development of social maturity is a long range goal, at best, and one which some would argue is secondary to those traditional goals that more closely reflect the cultural imperatives and personal growth. What of the more immediate, consensual goals of education and the impact of tutoring on these? Specifically, when students serve as tutors are they hindered or helped in measurable ways?

DOES TUTORING IMPROVE THE ACADEMIC SKILLS OF THE TUTORS?

A number of studies have examined this question. While not all have arrived at the same answer, results usually support the value of tutoring for tutors. Some studies have found that tutors benefit academically even more than the students whom they tutor (Morgan & Toy, 1970). Other studies have shown that tutors and learners profit equally from the experience (Mayhall, 1972), while a few have reported no benefit for tutors (Werth, 1968, cited in Cloward, 1976).

The Cloward Study

The most frequently cited report regarding the positive effects for tutors is that of Cloward (1967). Conducted under the auspices of Mobilization for Youth, a New York City antipoverty program, this large scale project produced findings so remarkable that they deserve closer examination. In this program high school students who were themselves lower achievers served as tutors for low achieving elementary students. The experiment was carefully designed, with random assignment of students to experimental (tutoring) and control (no tutoring) conditions from their respective age groups. Both the tutors and the learners achieved greater gains than their control groups. Tutored children registered moderate growth, advancing slightly over one month for each month in the program. The most astonishing effects, however, were reserved for the tutors, who gained nearly 5 months for every month in the program, a staggering 3.4 years advance in achievement over a 7 month span.

LEARNING ABOUT RESPONSIBILITY AND DEVELOPING SOCIAL MATURITY

Student Tutors Are Responsible

Elementary age students can be remarkably responsible about their teaching. I recently found a note in my school mailbox indicating that Lisa had called to say she might be late for tutoring because she had a dental appointment. By and large, tutors independently arrange another tutoring time for their students if special circumstances (e.g., a musical rehearsal) force a change in their daily schedule. *LMJ, Special Education Resource Teacher*

First Time Responsibility

Tutors do not have to be the top students in the class, although these students usually work well and can complete their own class work even though they spend a half hour out of the classroom each day. Often top students are shy, and tutoring helps them to develop self confidence. My most memorable experiences with tutors have been in working with students who are allowed to tutor as a reward for good work and behavior in other areas. Tutoring often gives students their first feelings of responsibility for another person. It may be the first time they have felt respected and trusted with an important responsibility. I'll never forget the beaming smiles of my "behavior disordered" students as they stepped forward in the awards assembly for their "super tutor" awards. *Ellen Pina, Special Education Teacher, Robeson School, Champaign, Illinois*

Mischief Among Tutors

Mischief among tutors is extremely rare. In my experience, tutors have been quite serious about their jobs and especially conscientious about remaining on task. On many occasions during tutoring I have left the room, or have had 8 to 10 visitors in the room simultaneously, or have had parents or other teachers stop in—and in none of those cases was the tutoring session interrupted. I suppose that a teacher might have problems if she rarely attended to and seldom supervised the tutors, but that would be asking for trouble. Another caution: I'd say that students who have severe behavior problems or are aggressive should not be placed with a cross age tutor. I worked with one very hard to teach youngster for a year and half before I felt comfortable in assigning him a tutor. Until that time, his lack of attending behaviors and reading skills made him a poor candidate for tutoring. Finally, in pairing tutors with students it is not advisable to pair youngsters who know each other too well. Larkin and Tony, two sixth grade boys, could not work together without arguing. Larkin resented the fact that his friend Tony "knew" more, and never accepted him as a teacher. *LMJ*

Good Citizen

Tutoring is well received in my school. In fact, serving as a tutor was included on one learning disabled student's IEP. Billy, a fifth grader, had lots of trouble in school both with teachers and with other students. It was hard for him to find anything positive about school. We decided that making Billy a tutor for another youngster might change his outlook. For the most part this worked well. Billy was responsible for behaving like a good citizen with his tutee, and this seemed to carry over to other situations as well. *Diane Goodwine, Special Education Resource Teacher, Leal School, Urbana, Illinois*

Establishing Confidentiality

Students want to be "professional" tutors. They learn that all discussions about a student between the resource teacher and tutor are private. Youngsters realize that they become privy to certain information that should not be discussed with their friends. For example, a tutor might be told: "I think Billy is sad about something happening at home. Please be extra careful to help him feel good about his academic accomplishments." Or "Midge makes lots of inappropriate verbal statements and this is causing a problem for her in the classroom and in the resource room. Try to ignore any bizarre talk and reinforce attending tasks and appropriate answers." As far as I know, my tutors have never abused this privilege. Tutors are quick to understand what is meant by professionalism. *LMJ*

Parental Response

I allow several children from my classroom to serve as tutors in our school's special education program. One might think that parents would be wary of their children's participation in this out of classroom activity. On the contrary, parents often thank me for allowing their child to participate in the tutoring program even though the child is out of the classroom each day. They also request that their child be recommended to the next teacher for continued tutoring opportunities. They are concerned parents who are pleased to see their child develop maturity, skills, self reliance, and pride in a job well done. *Nancy MacDonald, 4th Grade Teacher, Washington School, Champaign, Illinois*

Taken at face value, the Cloward study suggests that students can profit enormously from serving as tutors. However, the very magnitude of the reported achievement gains challenges the plausability of these findings. Specifically, it is difficult to believe that the tutors *learned* over 3 years worth of reading skills in a 7 month span and that this learning could be attributed to the experience of tutoring. Cloward himself recognized this problem and speculated that some portion of the apparent gains may have resulted from a testing artifact, since even the control group (other high school students) made unusually large achievement gains (1.7 months) during the same 7 month period. Quite possibly the pretest scores of both the tutors and their controls were depressed by the complexity of the test directions, such that on the posttest "a substantial portion of the increase for both groups may have been due to increased familiarity with the test directions" (Cloward, 1976, p. 223).

In addition to this explanation, tutoring itself may have affected test performance indirectly by altering the degree to which the tutors cooperated on the test. Low income high school students, many of whom are uninspired by school, can be notoriously difficult to test. Indeed, Cloward acknowledged that the "reading battery is rather long and *exceptionally difficult* to administer. . ." (p. 223, emphasis added). It is tempting to speculate that the students perceived the testing as a nuisance, failed to give their complete cooperation and performed on the pretest far beneath their actual achievement levels. Later, however, after a positive experience as tutors, they were more inclined to cooperate with the program organizers and perform their best on the posttests. Hence, they would provide a valid posttest score, but an inflated gain score due to their presumed failure to cooperate on the pretest. Of course, the control group students' motivation to perform on the posttests would have remained at its original low level, since these students had not undergone the tutoring experience.

Thus, there are several plausible interpretations for the large achievement gains of the tutors in Cloward's study, including increased test familiarity, increased cooperativeness by the tutor group on the achievement test, and, of course, an actual increase in achievement resulting from the tutoring experience. This study illustrates the difficulty encountered in ascribing achievement gains to specific causes. While the effects of tutoring itself were probably less staggering than first thought, at least partial credit for the actual achievement gains can be realistically attributed to the tutoring experience and taken as support for the proposition that children learn from teaching others.

Generalizations

Overall, two tentative generalizations are suggested by the findings on learning from tutoring. First, tutors appear more likely to make achievement gains when they work in unstructured programs where instructional content and the teaching methodologies must be invented by the tutor. This requires that the tutors themselves devote considerable time to studying the subject matter which may result in their reacquiring forgotten information through review, or reformulating previously acquired information into new knowledge structures. Gartner, Kohler, and Reissman (1971) commented:

> The process of reinforcing already learned knowledge itself has several dimensions. The child uses or works with the material several times: first, when initially learning it, perhaps some years ago; second, in reviewing it; third, in preparing it to teach to another; and, finally, in presenting it to the other child. And it is not only a simple matter of reviewing the material; in doing so one may reperceive it, may see it in new ways, perhaps synthesize it into new formulations, enriching one's knowledge of that material as well as material subsequently learned. (p. 60)

A second generalization about tutors is that they are more likely to show academic improvements when they are themselves somewhat deficient in the subject area tutored. Students who are already highly skilled in a subject matter (e.g., mathematics) are unlikely to become more proficient in the subject by teaching lower level aspects of the subject (e.g., counting). They might, however, learn something about teaching and about managing another's behavior.

What conclusions should teachers draw from these generalizations? Should teachers select low performing youngsters as their tutors and arrange for tutoring sessions free from structure? Perhaps, but some consideration must be given to the major purpose of the tutoring program, taking into account the minimal academic skills required to function as a successful tutor.

Selecting the Tutor

If the major intent of the program is to give needed systematic instruction to youngsters with academic problems, then teachers must be careful to select adequately skilled tutors, and to structure the tutoring situation so that it will definitely aid the learners. Some of the research that demonstrated academic benefits to the tutors did *not* show a similar benefit to the tutee. Indeed, these latter programs were designed to benefit the tutor, and in that they apparently succeeded.

One must be careful, however, in striving to create optimal benefits for the tutor, since the gains may be purchased at the learner's expense. Probably the most conservative approach is to select normal or high performing youngsters as tutors. A less conservative approach is to select low performing youngsters as tutors, but to employ them only with children who are much younger and much less skilled than themselves, or employ them with children whose needs are less urgent. We have observed the success of this latter approach on several occasions

19

when resource teachers have trained handicapped youngsters as tutors after they themselves had been tutored for a period of time.

As a study by Mayhall (1972) illustrates, certain tasks lend themselves to tutoring by children who are peers in the sense that both tutor and tutee are unskilled in the instructional objective. Mayhall sought to compare the relative benefits of tutoring and being tutored by selecting a learning objective upon which neither tutors nor tutees were competent. Prior to the study, all children were trained in tutoring skills: clear presentation, praising, appropriate prompting, and correcting. The learning task was math facts presented on flash cards with the answers lightly printed on the back of each flash card, allowing the tutor to give appropriate feedback.

Children alternated weekly between tutoring and being tutored. Learning measures were obtained at the end of each week. Mayhall found that in the weeks children served as tutors they increased their competence on math facts an amount equal to the increase they experienced during the weeks in which they were tutored. These results lend support to the dual benefits that accrue to both tutor and tutee and demonstrate how teachers may use academically unskilled children as tutors, provided that the task is carefully structured and allows the tutors access to the correct answers. Mayhall's research was corroborated by Dineen, Clark, and Risley (1977), who reported identical findings from a study that used spelling as the instructional content and classroom peers as tutors.

Are There Risks in Tutoring?

Occasionally, educators and parents are hesitant to let their children tutor because they fear the children will suffer academically if their own classroom time is reduced. However, the research on this issue suggests that their concerns may be relaxed. No study has given the slightest hint that tutors are academically harmed from their experience. On the contrary, more often than not tutors seem to grow academically more than their counterparts who do not tutor. Under the right circumstances even very able students may be exposed to and acquire new information. For example, a reading tutor may learn and encounter new and valuable information. Many reading selections that appear in contemporary basal series are on nonfiction topics drawn from the social or physical sciences. In addition, tutors who are properly trained learn certain behavioral principles that are the subject of psychology.

Teachers can minimize the risk that tutors will experience problems in the classroom by carefully scheduling the time when their students leave the room so they do not miss regular presentations, demonstrations, or discussions. Generally, classroom teachers who individualize and group for instruction can identify 30 minutes of "down time" in the morning or afternoon when selected students could engage in an extracurricular activity. Besides, most educators recognize that it is a

CHILDREN'S REACTIONS

Favorite Part of the Day

I enjoy tutoring a lot. I really look forward to it. It's my favorite part of the day. Some mornings I'll wake up and not want to go to school. Then I'll remember, David gets to start a new book today, or something like that, and I'll be excited all day! *Kara Mylerberg, 6th Grade Tutor, Franklin School*

Tutoring Conversations at Home

When report cards come out, I send a note to the tutors' parents regarding their performance. During a PTA meeting, a tutor's parents informed me that they were framing their son's Tutor Report Card for his room. The parents went on to say how they heard about the progress of their child's tutee every night at dinner. *Marianne Abbey, Title I Teacher, Garden Hills School, Champaign, Illinois*

Students Miss the Opportunity to Tutor

Our favorite babysitter, Angina Mittra, was a tutor for two years at Washington Elementary School in Champaign, Illinois. Later during Angina's junior high school years, she and her friends who also were extutors expressed disappointment that they no longer had an opportunity to tutor as junior high students. *LMJ, Special Education Resource Teacher*
One comment from one of my special education students that lingers in my mind: "Wouldn't it be neat if, after all this, we got to be tutors?" *Jan Walker, Special Education Teacher, Oregon, Illinois*

Students Enjoy Counting Behaviors

I remember Danny, a 6 year old, going home to report to his dad, a school board member, that he was "21" that day. Dad called to ask me what "21" meant as Danny was so proud. At that time I was consequating the number of pages he accurately read to his tutor, Yvette in a Sullivan workbook. The behavior was recorded on a "racetrack" poster. Danny was the first 1st grader to record a number in the twenties; and he was proud of this accomplishment. *LMJ*

Learning About Teaching

I think that being a tutor has helped me to understand the basics of teaching. Since I have always wanted to be a teacher it will be very easy for me to learn and work with kids. Tutoring is very exciting and besides just the fun of tutoring it has helped to prepare for my future. It has helped my attendance record. I used to like to be sick and miss school but now I want to be at school so I can tutor. *Lisa Parrott, 6th Grade Tutor, Ben Franklin School, Kirkland, Washington* rare student who can maintain a state of active learning throughout the length of an entire school day. Some teachers have used the opportunity to tutor as an incentive for motivating able students to execute their classroom assignments with proper diligence and efficiency.

Summary

At least four plausible explanations could be advanced to account for achievement gains by tutors. First, the experience of tutoring may serve as an occasion for students to acquire new information that they might not have encountered without training. For example, in helping a student with a reading lesson, tutors might be exposed to and assimilate information about the creation of fossils, the age and formation of our galaxy, the culture of the Navajos, the background and accomplishments of an historical figure, or how two children resolved a conflict. In tutor training sessions they may learn psychological concepts such as differential reinforcement, punishment, modeling, fading and shaping, and perhaps how these concepts apply to situations beyond those found in formal teaching arrangements.

Second, the act of tutoring may be an occasion for students to review and relearn information or skills that they have either forgotten or on which their proficiency had diminished. For example, tutoring content that includes vocabulary meanings, spelling words, math operations, and automatic math facts may pose opportunities for relearning or for upgrading previously acquired skills.

Third, tutors may become more conscientious about their own classroom work because they do not want to risk losing their tutoring privileges. They may even become more sensitive and reflective about their own behavior in their role of student once they have experienced the role of teacher.

Fourth, the opportunity to tutor may result in general attitudinal changes that indirectly influence the students' involvement in learning. For example, a successful experience in the role of tutor might raise some students' self confidence, prompting a shift in their appraisal of self as learner, and result in increased approach behaviors toward learning tasks from which they might once have been deterred. Or possibly, an enjoyable experience in tutoring might brighten a child's outlook and participation in school. It is a common event for classroom teachers and parents to spontaneously remark about the new enthusiasm their children have toward school after they have undertaken tutoring responsibilities.

Children who tutor appear in some cases to derive cognitive benefits from this addition to their school experience. If one were to discount the studies that show positive cognitive effects for tutors, then the experience of tutoring would appear to have, at worst, neutral effects on these students.

NONCOGNITIVE BENEFITS FOR TUTORS

The list of hypothesized noncognitive benefits to students who serve as tutors is quite long. Among the alleged benefits are increased altruism, empathy, self respect, ego strength, self esteem, self confidence, responsibility, sense of self accomplishment, maturity, seriousness of purpose, understanding of individual differences, improved attitudes toward school and adults, a new awareness about learning and studying, and the breaking down of racial prejudice (Gartner et al., 1971), and the development of social skills (Argyle, 1976). Although these are normally not listed among the primary goals of schooling along with increased knowledge and skills, many of them would qualify as subsidiary goals in the sense that they may help students attain the primary goals.

Research Findings

What is the evidence in regard to the noncognitive benefits of tutoring? Mostly positive. The experience of tutoring has seemingly paid dividends in a number of areas, including improved attitudes toward school, school subjects, and self concept (Haggerty, 1971; Jones, 1974; Mohan, 1972; Robertson, 1972; Symula, 1975; Yamamoto & Klentschy, 1972); level of aspiration (Elder, 1967); interracial integration and acceptance (Witte, 1972); personal confidence (Symula, 1975); and social adjustment (King, 1979). The results strongly favor tutoring. While several of the studies were exemplary, generalization from this research should be qualified since not all studies were true experiments and some used measurement devices that are subject to bias (e.g., teacher judgments about the effects on tutors). While the student tutors did cover a broad spectrum of age, 5th through 11th grades, they were primarily children who themselves had problems—e.g., underachievement, records of misbehavior, low popularity, poor motivation, negative attitudes, and poverty ridden environments. Many of the programs were designed, in fact, to compensate for these problems. In contrast, the effects of tutoring on more middle class, normally achieving youngsters are less understood. However, one might expect that factors responsible for positive effects on "problem" students would operate similarly for "nonproblem" students, although the needs of the latter might be less serious (e.g., motivation, self concept, etc.).

Why should tutoring produce such positive benefits for the tutor? Allen and Feldman (1976) proposed an explanation based on role theory:

> It is a basic tenet of role theory that enactment of a role produces changes in behavior, attitudes and self perceptions consistent with expectations associated with the role. [Moreover] Empirical data demonstrate that role enactment does indeed produce behavioral and attitudinal changes in the person enacting a

role...In the case of the child who enacts the role of teacher for another child, the role represents prestige, authority and feelings of competence; it would seem reasonable to expect that enacting the role of teacher would increase self-esteem and produce a more positive attitude toward school and teachers. (pp. 114-115)

By stepping into the teacher's shoes, a child qualifies for several desirable consequences including prestige in the eyes of peers, considerable attention and reinforcement from adults, and respect from the student who is tutored. Moreover, when tutors recognize that their younger students may imitate, emulate, and identify with them, they may even feel compelled to exhibit more socially desirable and appropriate behavior.

An additional benefit of tutoring suggested by Argyle (1976) is the development of both social and role taking skills. If social skills such as active listening; maintaining involvement; detecting and responding appropriately to another's mood, emotion, temperament, and level of understanding, etc., are learned as are physical skills through practice and modeling, then tutoring may contribute to their development by providing an opportunity for supervised practice.

Overall, the available research suggests that the opportunity to enact the role of teacher has a positive influence on children. Granted that some of this research has been weak and that it has often failed to include important populations (e.g., normally achieving, well adjusted, middle class youth), there appears to be no scientific evidence to suggest that children's academic, personal, or social development will be in some way impaired by this experience. On the contrary, the existing evidence supports an entirely opposite conclusion. Moreover, based on anecdotal reports, children and their parents who have experience in these programs are nearly always enthusiastic about them. Allen and Feldman (1976), for example, wrote that children participating in their tutoring programs "have expressed a very consistent and almost unanimous positive reaction," that older children "almost invariably have reported that they enjoyed teaching younger children," that the younger children "say that they like being taught in the one to one situation," and that students wanted to participate in these programs again in the future (p. 115). In our own experience, parents have reported that the opportunity to tutor was their children's favorite part of school and that they have voluntarily bused their children to magnet schools that hosted the tutoring program.

3 What Makes an Effective Tutoring Program?

One thing about tutoring is certain. It is not a new idea. Allen (1976) traced the history of child to child tutoring to the 18th century. Andrew Bell in India and later Joseph Lancaster in Britain made extensive use of children as teachers. Conditions in schools during this period differed dramatically from those of modern times. Classes were extremely large, often numbering more than 100, and were composed of students whose ages varied widely, often by as much as 10 or more years. The system developed by these men involved teacher led instruction of the oldest students, who then instructed younger students, and so on down the age and ability ranks. While the Bell-Lancaster system was widely disseminated and adopted by many, its necessity and popularity faded with increased public funding of schools and the growth of professional education. Since then child to child tutoring has turned up a number of times and even received large scale funding in the compensatory education programs of the 1960's. However, it has never managed to become a central and consistent instructional practice in the schools. In light of the frequently reported enthusiasm that accompanies tutoring programs, along with the usual impression of educational benefits, the impermanence of these programs is an interesting fact worthy of discussion and one which we will take up in the last chapter. But now we turn to a consideration of what makes some tutoring programs effective.

ELEMENTS OF AN EFFECTIVE TUTORING PROGRAM

Whether or not a program can be regarded as effective depends upon its goal. Tutoring programs have been devised to achieve a variety of goals. As noted earlier, some programs have focused on students as

25

tutors, intending to improve some aspect of their lives such as academic and interpersonal skills, and attitudes toward themselves, their peers, or school itself. When these programs have been evaluated, the primary outcome measures are cast in terms of tutor change. Of secondary concern was the effect that these programs had on the children who were tutored. In most cases, however, tutoring programs have been designed with the primary goal of helping the children who are tutored. For these programs, effectiveness is usually defined in terms of the extent to which they succeed in improving school achievement, a cultural imperative. Our discussion of factors related to program effectiveness will focus on this latter situation, where tutor or learner gain constitutes the outcome of interest.

PROGRAMED VS. DIRECTED TUTORING

While there have been many program evaluations of tutoring, relatively few were systematic attempts to determine the particular components needed to make a program effective. In some studies, one system of tutoring was contrasted with another; observed differences on outcome measure can sometimes help the practitioner select the more effective procedure. In other studies, a particular tutoring system was compared with nontutoring; regardless of the outcome, it is difficult to determine what specific aspects of the program are responsible for its success or failure, because any number of program components may have helped to produce the observed effects. Unfortunately, in most research on this topic tutoring has been compared with "not tutoring" rather than with another form of tutoring.

Even with the best research in the area, findings are not always crystal clear. An excellent study conducted by Ellson, Harris, and Barber (1968) illustrated the difficulties in drawing definite and unqualified conclusions about effective and noneffective tutoring procedures. This research contrasted Programed Tutoring with Directed Tutoring and with classroom instruction alone for first grade students from low income families. Programed Tutoring was characterized by specifically designed instructional content, which was derived from the Ginn Reading Series, along with highly prescribed instructional procedures for tutors to employ. All tutors followed identical steps in presenting stimuli, giving feedback, and requiring pre-established performance levels before allowing their students to proceed through the program (i.e., teaching to a mastery criterion).

In contrast, Directed Tutoring allowed far more flexibility in the selection of instructional content and procedures, and did not prescribe criterion levels for students. Still, content and procedures were not taken lightly, but were conscientiously designed by remedial reading teachers and reading specialists for application by the tutors. Included among the instructional materials were readiness books, the Ginn first grade series, Dolch word games, and supplementary reading stories. Classroom reading instruction for both of the tutoring conditions as well as for the nontutored classroom control group was based on the Ginn reading series.

In addition to these comparisons, the research provided information on the effect of one versus two daily 15 minute tutoring sessions. The study, which lasted an entire school year, produced extremely interesting results. Regular classroom instruction plus Directed Tutoring, which featured readiness activities, games, and enrichment lessons given on a daily basis, was no more effective than classroom instruction by itself. This finding came as a great surprise to all who had observed the Directed Tutoring sessions and prompted the authors to caution against evaluating the product of any tutoring program on the basis of its apparent effectiveness. Looks can be deceiving! According to Ellson, et al.,

> In operation, Directed Tutoring seemed more than satisfactory: the children appeared to be learning and to enjoy the tutoring sessions. Their teachers generally approved of the tutoring activities. The tutors were enthusiastic about their work and close personal relationships with the children tutored were very apparent. Both tutors and those who observed them had no doubts that a real contribution was being made to the children's reading skills...

> But the favorable impression of Directed Tutoring as a teaching procedure was not supported by evidence that it improved reading achievement... This suggests the need for caution in evaluating any such program on the basis of apparent good teaching practice rather than hard achievement data. (p. 343, emphasis added)

In contrast, the children receiving Programed Tutoring twice daily made highly significant achievement gains. Notably, only one session per day of Programed Tutoring did not discernibly improve the children's achievement relative to classroom instruction alone.

The research by Ellson, et al. has high face validity inasmuch as it was conducted in several elementary schools, with many children participating in each condition, lasted for a full school year, and used as its instructional content materials and procedures that are commonly available to teachers. The finding that two daily 15 minute tutoring sessions affected achievement, but that one session did not, has clear implications for structuring the length or duration of tutoring. Also important was the rather startling finding that an entire year of Directed Tutoring did not help the children read better; it demonstrated that merely increasing instructional time will not necessarily boost learning and that tutoring must be structured appropriately before it will result in the intended effects. Another important finding is that both observations of tutoring and self reports by tutors and learners may be quite misleading. Recall that observers and participants gave glowing reports of the Directed Tutoring treatment, which was later found to be ineffective. This suggests a need for careful monitoring of children's learning to assure that apparent successes have some basis in reality.

On the other hand, it is not altogether clear which particular components of Programed Tutoring were responsible for the impressive results obtained by this intervention. It might be that a systematic sequence was followed, guaranteeing repetition and review of instructional content. Another possibility was that the content of tutoring was consistent with the content of classroom instruction in that both followed the Ginn reading series. Teaching to mastery, which characterized programed tutoring, may have been another factor responsible for this program's success, because children had to read each word and sentence correctly before they could proceed through the program. In contrast, the lessons in Directed Tutoring did not adhere to any particular sequence (so review was not guaranteed), the lessons were not closely tied to the classroom reading series, and children were not taught to mastery. Instead, one day they might play word bingo, the next day practice letters, and the next day interpret picture stories.

The point is that even this excellent experiment by Ellson, et al., although providing important evidence on certain questions, still leaves a number of other questions unresolved. With that caveat, we will turn to an examination of what research and experience suggest about structuring tutoring programs. Among the questions considered are those relating to content of instruction, measurement procedures, frequency and duration of tutoring, mastery requirements, program organizations, tutor training and supervision, and tutor selection and pairing with learners.

CONTENT OF INSTRUCTION

With respect to instructional content or what is taught, tutor programs have taken a number of widely varying approaches, ranging from content selected to be highly correlated with the child's classroom programs (Ellson, et al. 1968; Jenkins & Mayhall, 1979), to content that is determined basically by the tutor (Mobilization for Youth, 1959, described in Gartner, Kohler, & Reissman, 1971), to content constructed especially for tutoring, but independent of the child's classroom program (Smith, 1975). Selecting instructional content depends to some extent on program goals. The Mobilization for Youth program was primarily intended to influence the achievement and attitudes of tutors rather than their students. The decision to allow tutors to select instructional content was deliberately made, under the presumption that this would help tutors develop self confidence, enthusiasm for teaching, and interest in school. As noted earlier, however, tutoring programs are more often developed for those who are tutored, and under these circumstances, it makes little sense to adopt a laissez faire attitude toward the content of instruction within an important remedial service.

28

The Merits of Various Tutoring Contents.

Few systematic comparisons have been reported on the relative merits of different instructional contents. The work by Ellson, et al. (1968) was closest to a study of different contents, but in their research directed and programed tutoring conditions differed on other factors as well, e.g. teaching to mastery. Yet, Ellson, et al. believed that the close correspondence between the contents of programed tutoring and the classroom reading series (Ginn) was a significant factor in the success of this intervention.

Although there is little scientific evidence to recommend correlating tutoring content with classroom content, there are some common sense notions that support such a practice. In the first place, the concepts of normalization and least restrictive environment impact on the design of special education programs that offer classroom support and remedial services. These concepts imply that services for children with learning handicaps should be designed in ways that assist the children to maintain their enrollment in normal school settings. Most often these are regular education classrooms that include nonhandicapped agemates. Unfortunately, when children with learning problems cannot keep up with their classmates, their teachers are inclined to dispatch them to another setting, one from which they rarely return. Thus, the challenge for special and remedial teachers is to help the children demonstrate that they can satisfy the major program objectives of the regular classroom and can remain a part of the mainstream.

Since regular education teachers usually define program objectives in terms of their classroom curricula, they tend to judge children's competence in relation to success or failure in those materials. Following this line of reasoning, special and remedial education teachers need to ensure that their efforts result in children's satisfactory performance in the classroom teacher's curriculum. However, different curricula have been shown to vary greatly in their contents. The skills and words taught in one series may have very little overlap with those taught in another series. For example, Barnard and DeGracie (1976) found that the *majority* of words taught in any one major basal series during the first grade are *not* taught in other major series during first grade. Similar results were reported by Jenkins and Pany (1978), who noted that certain reading series tended to correspond quite closely with particular achievement tests, but that other series did not, again indicating substantial differences in content between reading programs.

Nor are curriculum differences confined to the teaching of specific vocabulary; they include comprehension skills as well. Armbruster, Stevens, and Rosenshine (1977) compared third grade workbooks from the Ginn, Economy, and Houghton-Mifflin series. They found that the relative emphasis on specific reading comprehension exercises (e.g., drawing conclusions and cloze) varied substantially across the three series, with emphasis given to different skills by any two of the series correlating on the average at only 0.33.

This research suggests that remedial services based on the child's classroom curriculum will more likely improve performance in that curriculum. In contrast, services based on another curriculum, even if they effectively teach that curriculum's objectives, are less likely to teach the "right" skills—i.e., those the classroom teacher uses as his or her criterion. Based on their research, Barnard and DeGracie (1976) drew a similar conclusion: "Since beginning reading vocabularies are significantly different, it appears that the student would benefit from using one basal system until the decoding process is mastered. If teachers feel the need to supplement, it would probably be better to purchase the supplemental readers provided with most systems" (p. 180).

CURRICULUM SELECTION

Transfer to the Classroom

In my fifth year of teaching, I was assigned a second grade class of 21 students; approximately one-third of them received remedial reading and/or math instruction in the special education resource room. For the *first* time in my teaching experience, the supportive services of a special education program had a noticeable impact on my students' performance and progress. I'm referring not just to gains on year end achievement tests, but rather to day to day differences; children participated more in reading group activities, seat work assignments, oral reading, and recitation of math facts. I'm sure that many components of the special education program contributed to students' gains (e.g., systematic data collection and monitoring of student performance; one to one instruction from cross age tutors; the resource teacher's expertise in designing instruction; and her genuine interest in each student). Her choice of curriculum, however, made the largest contribution to improving students' classroom performance. Unlike other special education programs I have been involved with, this one used *my* reading books, *my* phonics sequence, *my* math program, and *my* spelling words. In that way, students received instruction that was compatible with their classroom programs. For that reason, I regarded the resource teacher as my teaching partner. The outcome was fantastic! *Darlene Pany, Former 2nd Grade Teacher*

Jenny, a fifth grade tutor, gave Donald, her student, a written award for completing Level 9 with mastery. Mrs. Henry read the award to the class and praised Donald. Because the reading curriculum used in the resource room was the same as that in the classroom, Donald, his classmates, the teacher, and Jenny all "understood" what completing Level 9 meant. Since Level 10 was the "lowest" level used for any reading group in this classroom, Donald could finally participate in a classroom reading group. *LMJ, Special Education Resource Teacher*

In extreme cases, certain curricula may not only lack correspondence but even be incompatible with each other and are, therefore, capable of confusing children. For example, some arithmetic operations are taught using different algorithms (e.g., counting down versus counting up to supply a missing addend), which can create problems for the novice, especially those who are experiencing difficulty learning in the first place. In reading, one program might use a modified orthography (e.g., Distar and ITA) to denote particular sound/symbol relationships, whereas another program uses standard orthographies. Or one program might confine first grade decoding instruction to short vowels (e.g., Sullivan) while another introduces both long and short vowels (e.g., Lippincott). Thus, the argument for basing tutoring support services on children's classroom curricula has obvious face validity, especially in the case of children receiving special education services, as they are in jeopardy of removal from the regular education program.

On the other side of the coin, using regular classroom curriculum materials can sometimes prove impractical—for example, when they are plagued by major design inadequacies or when children cannot perform satisfactorily in them even with tutoring. In reading, the likelihood of needing a curriculum change increases when the classroom has employed a whole word program with insufficient phonic support.

What, then, should dictate the choice of tutoring content? The dangers inherent in moving to nonsequential, noncumulative tutoring content were evident in the results of Ellson, et al.'s Directed Tutoring condition. When tutoring lessons skipped about from activity to activity, producing mastery on none, the tutoring program produced no discernible effects on students' achievement, even though it was given daily for an entire year.

One alternative to the high risk, nonsequential program is to select another standard reading series, presumably one more suited to a student's needs. A second alternative is to select from a number of made for tutoring programs such as *Sounder* (Smith, 1975), Structured Tutoring (Harrison, 1971), or the Monterey Tutoring Program. Either alternative has its advantages. With the first, chances are greater that the curriculum selected by the remedial program may ultimately replace the child's original classroom curriculum. This would depend on the regular classroom teacher's willingness to employ more than one series in his or her program, and to define grade level programs according to accomplishments in a second curriculum series. The advantage of adopting a made for tutoring program is that content, lessons, presentation formats, correction procedures, and proficiency levels for advancement have been precisely detailed. However, it is unlikely that the regular classroom program can be coordinated with the remedial tutoring program.

While the research on instructional content is not altogether conclusive, there is at least some certainty about what *not* to teach. The use of differential diagnostic-prescriptive teaching (DD-PT) approaches, sometimes referred to as process approaches, are prevalent within many special education programs and to a lesser extent within remedial education programs. Under these approaches, which Haring and Bateman (1977) have referred to as the majority position in learning disabilities, children with learning problems are given intensive perceptual-motor and "psycholinguistic" programs such as those advocated by Frostig and Horne (1964), Kephart (1960), and Minskoff (1975). Usually these programs attempt to strengthen some underlying psychological ability like eye-hand coordination, spatial relations, laterality, body image, auditory reception, or visual sequential memory, and thereby improve the youngsters' ability to acquire ordinary academic skills in which learning is presumed to have been hindered because of the underlying ability weakness.

Arter and Jenkins (1979) reviewed the literature on the efficacy of DD-PT. They found that in the well controlled studies that attempted to improve underlying ability weaknesses through direct ability training (e.g., with Frostig training procedures) less than 24% proved successful, and only 29% reported some carryover benefits to academic areas. Further, Arter and Jenkins identified other important problems with this model; namely, that many instruments used for differential diagnosis lack adequate reliability and validity to justify their use in educational programs for children.

The research on DD-PT has two important implications for tutoring programs. First, teachers would probably be unwise to design lessons for tutors that are derived from this model. That is, instructional content should stick to the basics—those skills and knowledge domains ordinarily taught in regular classrooms. Second, some special education teachers might be reluctant to employ cross age tutors or other volunteers in their programs because these people lack training in sophisticated diagnostic procedures and complex prescriptive methodologies. Given the consistent research support for cross age tutoring and the consistently negative research findings related to the DD-PT model, these teachers probably should not relax their concern. They might effectively upgrade their programs by adding tutors and subtracting the DD-PT components.

ESTABLISHING MASTERY LEVELS

Closely related to the issue of instructional content is the degree to which a tutoring program approximates a mastery learning model. At issue is whether tutoring will be primarily activity and process centered, or learning and mastery centered. The ineffective Directed Tutoring condition in the Ellson et al. (1968) experiment was a classic example of an activity oriented program. Tutors did not follow step by step procedures, presenting new material only after old material was mastered. Rather, their focus was more on teaching than on learning. Student mastery of objectives did not dictate what tutors would teach on ensuing lessons. For example, one lesson might focus on consonant blends, the next lesson might feature a word lotto game, and the next be chiefly devoted to word meanings, regardless of the student's performance. In contrast, a mastery model assumes that any skills targeted for instruction are of sufficient importance to require that students demonstrate mastery of them.

In a mastery based tutoring model, skills (e.g., a set of letter sounds) are identified and instruction occurs every day on that same skill until students achieve mastery. For example, new letter sounds are not introduced until previously taught sounds are learned. Usually very precise learning criteria are established for every skill, guaranteeing that instruction will continue until the criteria are met. Ellson, et al.'s programed tutoring condition, which proved highly effective, applied mastery learning procedures. Students' progress through the skill sequence was dictated by attainment of prior objectives.

Since no experiments have directly compared a teaching to mastery approach with an activity centered approach, it would be unwarranted to draw a definitive conclusion on this issue and require adoption of a mastery model. The Ellson et al. study clearly favored the tutoring program that used a mastery model over the activity oriented program, but contents also differed in these two programs. Based on our own survey of tutoring research, we have noted that successful programs have usually adopted a mastery orientation. For example, Robertson (1972), who used fifth grade students as tutors for poor performing first graders, Neidermeyer and Ellis (1971), who used fifth and sixth grade students as tutors for kindergarten children, and Jenkins and Mayhall (1979), who used older students as tutors of learning disabled and mentally retarded youngsters, all employed a mastery model that prescribed specific content and performance criteria for progress. In contrast, some other tutoring programs failed to demonstrate any benefits for the tutored children and a number of these programs chose a more laissez faire, activity centered approach. In addition to Ellson et al., other examples of unsuccessful tutoring programs that adopted this more relaxed practice include studies by Kelly (1972) and Foster (1972).

Although the topic has not been studied, the tutors' satisfaction with and sense of accomplishment from their jobs may be affected by the opportunity to observe their students actually master the instructional content. Presumably, one of the more potent intrinsic reinforcers connected with teaching is the sense of accomplishment that comes with having discernibly helped someone. Learning is more readily observed in a mastery model than in an activity centered model, because in the mastery model students remain on a single task for several days until they have attained it. We support the idea that tutors who work in

33

a mastery model will derive greater satisfaction from their tutoring, because they will be witness to the changes in their students' performance.

In addition to the evidence gleaned from research, conventional wisdom suggests the importance of carefully selecting tutoring content and guaranteeing that students master the content. It stands to reason that programs focusing on the "wrong" content will not help students much, even if they succeed in teaching that content. Likewise, tutoring programs emphasizing "right" content will also fail, if they do not guarantee that children acquire and master this content.

FREQUENCY AND DURATION OF TUTORING LESSONS

One of the first considerations in implementing a tutoring program is the scheduling of instructional sessions. How long should each session last and how many days per week should tutoring occur? Evidence from studies of academic engaged time and class size would suggest the more the better, at least up to the point of fatigue. However, other considerations will often dictate decisions about the frequency and duration of tutoring. For example, time available for tutoring may be greatly affected by the choice of tutors, e.g., adults, children, volunteers, or employees, and by their competing responsibilities and the budget constraints of the program.

Only two studies have directly investigated the scheduling factor. One was the previously described Ellson, et al. (1968) study in which two daily 15 minute sessions were compared with a single 15 minute session. Achievement results indicated that only the double sessions were effective. Even the highly successful Programed Tutoring condition produced inconspicuous gains when it was scheduled only once daily for 15 minutes, suggesting that very short sessions may not be worth the effort.

Frequency of tutoring was the subject of a study by Mayhall and Jenkins (1974), who compared short daily sessions with longer, twice weekly sessions for learning disabled youngsters. Their findings indicated that children learned more under the daily schedule even though total tutoring time was equal for both conditions. Taken together, the studies by Ellson, et al. and Jenkins and Mayhall suggest that tutoring will be more effective when scheduled daily and for sessions that last approximately half an hour.

Some writers have cautioned against daily sessions, speculating that boredom will occur and diminish the positive benefits of a tutoring program. Our experience does not support this view. Both tutors and the children tutored have maintained their enthusiasm for this activity for not only a single academic year, but over the course of 3 full years. Some antidotes to boredom and lassitude include an occasional change of tutor-learner pairings, scheduling reinforcing events for both tutors and learners, and making the job of tutoring prestigious in the school. Shaver and Nuhn (1968) have also conducted a long term tutoring program using the same paid adults over a 3 year period.

Other considerations, although not data based, favor scheduling daily sessions of moderate length. One consideration is the classroom disruption produced by children departing for the tutoring site and the additional teacher energies consumed in organizing this extra transition. To justify this, tutoring sessions should last long enough to have an effect and not just result in extra bother. A second consideration is especially pertinent in programs using cross age tutors from the school. Classroom teachers often prefer a fixed time, a regular (daily) schedule when their students will be out of the room for tutoring. This allows them to plan for and concentrate their efforts exclusively on the remaining students.

It would be misleading to imply that a tutoring program *must* be scheduled daily for approximately half hour sessions if it is to be effective. On the contrary, a number of successful tutoring programs have employed a less than daily schedule, or one with individual sessions lasting under 30 minutes (Harrison, 1971; Niedermeyer & Ellis, 1971; Klosterman, 1970). Our point is that when temporal factors were studied experimentally, results favored the longer, more continuous programs. This in combination with nuisance factors, such as interruption of classroom schedules and transition time, points to daily sessions of moderate length as the preferred organization, as long as other factors, such as availability of tutors, do not dictate otherwise.

TUTOR TRAINING AND SUPERVISION

The last thing teachers want to create is an unpleasant and negative interpersonal experience for children. Researchers have observed that if left to their own, older children will occasionally show impatience, or boss and ridicule younger children whom they are "helping" (Lippitt, 1968); nor is such behavior limited to children. To prevent this situation, it is essential that tutors be trained in appropriate interpersonal behaviors that will result in a comfortable and satisfying experience for both members of the tutoring dyads.

In addition to the obvious need to provide tutors with directions pertaining to the content of instruction, conventional wisdom about good instructional practices suggests several behaviors that tutors should be trained to perform. For example, teachers and tutors should give clear directions, encourage and praise learners for their efforts, confirm correct responses, correct errors in a nonpunitive fashion, and avoid overprompting. Interestingly, children who tutor appear not to engage in these behaviors spontaneously, according to a study by Niedermeyer (1970). Fifth and sixth grade students, who had received no specific tutor training, tended during tutoring sessions to confirm correct responses less than 50% of the time, rarely gave corrective feedback, and did not praise their tutees. Moreover, they did not engage in friendly, noninstructional conversation before or after the tutoring sessions. In contrast, tutors who had

35

received training in these behaviors exhibited high rates of appropriate instructional and interpersonal behavior.

Research conducted on the teaching styles of children indicates substantial individual differences among youngsters in their delivery of positive and negative consequences during instruction. Feshbach (1976) has noted that children's tendency to provide positive or negative feedback to other children in the form of verbal and nonverbal cues is related to such factors as the tutor's socioeconomic class, race, maternal reinforcement style, and cognitive/achievement competence. Thus, while some children may approach the tutoring role with interpersonal and social skills, others will need training and careful supervision, lest they produce negative learning conditions that interfere not only with effective transmission of information, but also with the learner's enjoyment, motivation, and self evaluation.

These and several other tutoring skills—such as placing learners in an instructional sequence; procedures for teaching letter names, letter sounds, and sound blending; and record keeping practices—were included in the tutor training program developed by Harrison (1969). To determine the value of this training, Harrison compared the learning of children taught by trained tutors with others taught by untrained tutors. His results strongly favored the group taught by trained tutors in that these children learned more, even though instructional time was equal for both groups. In a related study, Osguthorpe and Harrison (1976) concluded that role playing the tutoring skills during the training sessions was important to the success of the program. In this study, parent-tutors who had practiced the tutoring skills in role playing situations produced larger learning gains than either parents who received no training or those who had read a manual and observed tutoring demonstrations.

What do these findings suggest for teachers? Although only a few studies have addressed the issue of tutor training directly, these have produced reasonably consistent findings in favor of training. Some general skills that cut across a number of instructional tasks include giving clear direction, confirming correct responses, applying nonpunitive corrections, praising the tutee for appropriate behavior, and friendly conversing before and after the tutoring sessions. Efficiency considerations also suggest that tutors be trained in gathering and replacing their instructional materials, measuring and recording student performance, allocating time to specific tasks, and possibly monitoring or participating in posttutoring games the student may have earned. Other tutoring tasks such as teaching letter sounds, blending, sounding out, counting, arithmetic algorithms, and specialized correction procedures will require specific training if a tutor is assigned to teach them. Moreover, it is probably wise to remember that training need not end once actual tutoring begins. Careful supervision of the tutors will alert teachers to additional training needs.

The need for proper supervision was demonstrated in a study by

Mayhall, Jenkins, Chestnut, Rose, Shroeder, and Jordan (1975). The intent of this research was to examine both setting and supervisory factors in a cross age tutoring program for learning disabled children. In the first experiment, tutoring was conducted in the students' regular classrooms or in the special education resource room. In both settings minimal supervision was given by the teacher in charge. No differences were observed in the amount students learned in the different settings. The second experiment was identical to the first except that the resource room teacher actively monitored, encouraged, and guided the tutors. As in the first study, the classroom teacher taught a small group of classmates during the tutoring sessions, and thus provided minimal supervision of the tutors. The children who were taught by the closely supervised tutors learned more over the same period than did their counterparts in the classroom.

Taken together, these findings suggest that supervision adds significantly to the effects of tutoring, and that the location of tutoring is less critical. However, as these researchers noted, it is often difficult to structure carefully supervised tutoring in the regular classroom because teachers usually must perform other functions that are incompatible with supervising. Of course, if a teacher arranged for all the children in the classroom to receive tutoring simultaneously, he or she would be more able to supply the necessary supervision.

An alternative is for the classroom teacher to delegate supervisory responsibilities to someone else—for example, a teacher aide, another student, or the special education teacher. One drawback to this arrangement is that the often significant noise produced by the tutoring groups may interfere with the lessons and private work of the other children. Unless regular classroom teachers are prepared to make a strong commitment to organizing a tutoring program, including training and supervising the tutors, it is probably advisable for another professional (a resource, consulting, or remedial teacher) to assume the management responsibility and to locate the program in his or her own setting.

MEASUREMENT OF PROGRESS

One obvious disadvantage of turning over instructional duties to another person is that teachers may relinquish a certain amount of their intimate knowledge about how their students are progressing. When teachers themselves conduct a lesson, they have many opportunities to observe and assess how children are progressing. They can identify which children need additional practice, which children need more challenging material, and which ones are becoming discouraged, inattentive, or confused. With this information teachers can make appropriate program adjustments. However, when they establish a tutoring program, teachers give up some of this minute to minute monitoring ability.

One means of compensating for this information loss is to be present during tutoring and observe the teaching-learning activities. The previously mentioned study by Mayhall, et al. (1975) indicated that such supervision can make an important difference in a program's success. However, as Ellson, et al. (1968) pointed out, appearances are sometimes misleading, and what passes for effective tutoring under informal observations may not prove effective when actual learning measures are examined.

The contribution of a data system to instructional decision making has been the subject of several experiments. In one study, Jenkins, Mayhall, Peschka, and Townsend (1974) compared relative learning when cross age tutors measured children's performance either daily or not at all. The teachers who had access to the daily measures were able to make better program adjustments that resulted in greater learning by the learning disabled students who were being tutored. Although they did not conduct their studies in tutoring programs, Bohannon (1975) and Mirkin (1978) found similar effects when special education teachers used daily data to make instructional decisions.

In our experience, we have found that tutors can learn to collect daily performance data on each teaching objective. For example, within a reading lesson that includes instruction on letter sounds, isolated words, reading in context, and comprehension questions, the tutor will measure each element separately and display the results visually on a chart. By inspecting these charted performances, teachers determine how each child is progressing on each task, when instructional procedures need to be changed, and when the child is ready for a new task. Tutors are usually enthusiastic about measuring and charting performance; it not only provides evidence of their own effectiveness, but also constitutes one of the "special teaching skills" that makes the role of tutor distinctive.

One last word about measuring learner performance. The primary reason for establishing a systematic means of monitoring student progress is to supply teachers with valid information on their students' learning. In a sense, these measures are a way for the practitioner to keep his or her fingers on the patient's pulse and to take corrective action when a problem is detected. The measurement procedures should be objective, especially if the tutors are to conduct the assessments. Tutors should not, however, be placed in the position of grading their students or of making judgments regarding the adequacy and quality of their work. That is the teacher's job. Tutors dislike their jobs when they are placed in an evaluative role. They find this task particularly unpleasant when rewards to their student are contingent upon their evaluative judgments (Towson & Allen, 1970). Thus, while we believe that a measurement system is essential and recommend that tutors administer the measures, we strongly suggest that the measures be entirely objective (e.g., percent correct on a word list or correct math facts per minute) and that teachers be careful to distinguish between the measurement responsibilities they give to tutors and the evaluative responsibilities they reserve for themselves.

These findings support the common sense notion that decision making improves when people have access to better information, a proposition that is as true in classrooms as it is in government and industry. In addition to their contribution to decision making, good data systems can have other beneficial effects as well. In tutoring programs it is especially important to keep both tutors and learners focused on particular outcomes. When students recognize that their progress toward specific objectives will be measured at the end of every day's lesson, they are less likely to drift off task. In addition to this focusing function, performance measures also provide both partners in tutoring dyads with hard and satisfying evidence on the fruits of their labor. Finally, the data gathered on tutoring outcomes can be useful to program organizers in justifying the continuation and expansion of this service.

TAKING ON THE ROLE OF TEACHER

Measurement Is Important to Tutors

Being a tutor who used data based instruction is important. I had a fifth grade tutor who said to me, "How could someone teach reading without keeping charts and daily records?" I remember thinking I wish the graduate students assigned to me for practicum had the same insight. Using observable, countable, and measurable behaviors allows tutors to evaluate their success as a teacher. Lisa's mother remarked that her daughter gave daily reports on the number of sounds her student could do.

My tutors love carrying their stopwatches around their necks when picking up their students and showing off their performance charts to teachers and parents. Whenever an open house is held in my school, the tutors bring their parents in to show their instructional materials and charts, and to teach their parents how to use the calculator to compute percent and rate correct. I frequently have more tutor families than my students' families visit my room. *LMJ, Special Education Resource Teacher*

Teachers Need to Be Good Models

The "tutor teacher," as my tutors always refer to me, needs to model good instructional behaviors since tutors are quick to imitate what they observe. When I listen to my tutors I hear the same phrases, "good remembering," "great sounding," and even my tone of voice. Because I will often give students written awards for completing books or an especially good lesson, my tutors now do this as well. In fact, their awards are usually more creative than mine! *LMJ*

39

Melaragno (1976) has identified three types of program organizations for tutoring: intergrade, interschool, and within class. Under an intergrade tutoring program, older classes of students are paired with younger classes, sometimes on a schoolwide basis. With interschool tutoring, students from a nearby school act as tutors for younger students in the latter's school building. Instances of interschool programs include senior high school students tutoring junior high or elementary students, and junior high students serving as tutors in elementary schools.

Interschool and sometimes intergrade tutoring require the services of a program manager. School psychologists might serve effectively in this capacity. The third organization, within class tutoring, may involve either pairing advanced or "expert" students with slower learners from the same room, or sometimes pairing near ability students in memorizing or drill-like tasks. One obvious requirement in the near ability pairings is the selection of suitable learning tasks. Because certain tasks require that one person (the tutor) has already acquired the target skill (sight words, oral reading, arithmetic operations), they are not well suited for near ability tutoring pairs—the proverbial problem of the blind leading the blind. Other tasks such as spelling practice, word meaning instruction, and math fact drill can be structured so that the "tutor" has access to the answers, and both parties can take turns being the tutor.

To the organizations described by Melaragno we would add a fourth, special services tutoring, to identify the situation where a tutoring program is created and managed by a special education resource consulting teacher or a remedial education teacher. In keeping with our orientation in this book of focusing on programs for hard to teach children, we will devote more attention to special services tutoring, although fully recognizing that the larger scale, schoolwide programs outlined by Melaragno can have an enormous impact on children's achievement. More often than not, however, schoolwide tutoring programs are created because they seem to be a good idea rather than out of a sense of urgency. They tend to place high demands on the teachers and program coordinator, requiring cooperation and commitment to an "extracurricular" activity which can come to be perceived as an unnecessary burden. For these reasons, most schoolwide tutoring programs have trouble getting off the ground, and once established, tend to have a short life expectancy. Special services tutoring, in contrast, is more easily organized and managed, places fewer demands and burdens on classroom staff, is less disruptive to ongoing classroom programs, and does not require total commitment and involvement from the entire school community.

Special services tutoring programs run on a smaller scale but borrow ingredients from both intergrade and interschool programs. As is the case in intergrade programs, older students are selected from upper grades to tutor younger handicapped students under the supervision of a special teacher. Like interschool programs, special services programs sometimes enlist the services of students from nearby schools. Haynes (1977), for example, arranged for senior high students to enroll in a "teaching" course for credit in which they provided daily tutoring services in reading and spelling for learning disabled youngsters at a nearby junior high school. Special education consulting teachers in Vermont created a similar program for high school students who tutored elementary age handicapped students in arithmetic (Armstrong, et al., 1979).

Teachers, other than special education resource teachers and remedial education teachers, can take advantage of tutors' help. A regular classroom teacher might design a small scale tutoring program for some of his or her hard to teach children as a means of supporting them in the educational mainstream. Likewise, teachers in self contained special education classrooms can strengthen their instructional program by importing tutors from regular classrooms. In either case, the classroom teacher must set aside time to train the tutors, identify appropriate lessons, devise a measurement system, and incorporate tutoring into the regular classroom schedule. Several obstacles confront teachers who select this option. They must find time to train and confer with their tutors, schedule activities for their other children during the tutoring time, and manage the activities of all children in the room. None of these obstacles are insurmountable, however. When available, an aide or parent volunteer can lend assistance by conducting a group lesson for the other children or by helping them with their private seat work, for example. To avoid conflicts with other classroom obligations, the classroom teacher might consider scheduling tutor training and debriefing sessions during nonclassroom hours, such as recess, lunch period, or after school.

SELECTING TUTORS AND PAIRING THEM WITH LEARNERS

Since almost no research has addressed this issue, teachers have had little choice but to rely on their intuitions both in selecting tutors and in pairing tutors with learners. With availability dictating the pool of potential tutors, it has not always been possible for teachers to follow their natural preference for older, academically competent student tutors; nevertheless, in many cases teachers have been able to design high quality programs using children as young as 7, 8, and 9. As a general rule, however, older, more able students are the first choice because they are easier to train, require less supervision, and are better able to manage discipline problems than are younger tutors.

Academically capable fifth and sixth grade students make ideal tutors; they are often available because they have little trouble meeting the challenges at their grade levels and consequently can complete their assignments independently. Often, they are willing to buckle down and use their classroom study time efficiently to complete their

SELECTING CHILDREN AS TUTORS

Many Children Aspire to Be Tutors

A number of my children who were tutored by older students held aspirations to become tutors themselves. I trained two fourth grade boys, who were originally tutored in reading, to be math tutors; they tutored each other on multiplication facts. They were then included in tutor breakfasts, lunches, and the end of the year party. The academically high achieving youngsters welcomed the "special education" students as tutors. In fact, I never had to "explain" their presence. Normally, I try to have tutoring fairly well established before introducing special education youngsters as tutors, although recently I included a "tutored" youngster in the first batch of tutors at one school, and he has done quite well. *LMJ*

Are Peers Viable Tutors?

In my 8 years of managing tutoring programs I've always preferred using older students as tutors, but on several occasions I have used peers. In one instance, Lucy, a second grader in San Miguel Elementary School, made more academic gains and liked tutoring better after her classmate Hortense became her tutor. This particular pairing lasted for the entire school year. *LMJ*

Special Education Students as Tutors

Rick is a sixth grader who receives special services in math. He also tutors another sixth grader on multiplication and division facts. Since tutoring Michael, Rick's rate on multiplication facts has gone from 7 per minute to 28 per minute in 8 weeks. *LMJ*

Different Tutoring Benefits for Different Children

When I recommend children to be tutors, I think about their different needs. Each tutor becomes personally involved with another human being's frustrations and successes. Like many who tutor, Jennifer improved her own comprehension skills and level of self confidence. Cindy, who had been argumentative and snippy with peers, learned to be more tolerant and patient. Brock learned to concentrate, make a commitment to a task, and control his tendencies to play when the teacher's back was turned. Matthew learned to organize his time and work. Each child in my class considers tutoring an earned and treasured privilege. *Nancy MacDonald, 4th Grade Teacher, Washington School, Champaign, Illinois*

One Classroom Teacher's Criteria for Recommending Children as Tutors

I look for the following kinds of traits when I recommend children to be tutors:

1. Hard working students because children who are conscientious in class will probably be conscientious tutors. Also, they usually have to work for their grades. I tend to avoid recommending some of the brilliant kids since they sometimes don't have much empathy for those who don't have all the answers.
2. First child from a loving family, since they have experience in nurturing their siblings.
3. Children from a large family because they too are accustomed to helping others. I sometimes avoid the youngest of a large family if he appears too self centered (spoiled). *Kay Hendrick, 5th - 6th Grade Teacher, Audubon School, Redmond, Washington*

Not For Everyone

I've used several LD students as tutors. And this has worked out very well, with only one exception. One LD student (who had a behavior problem as well) couldn't handle the responsibility. I'm hoping that he might try again at a later time. *Diane Goodwine, Special Education Resource Teacher, Leal School, Urbana, Illinois*

Another Viewpoint on Selecting Tutors and Tutees

As a Title I reading teacher, I have used a peer tutoring program for the last 3 years. Approximately one third of my case load is involved with the peer tutoring program.

In deciding which children will be tutored, there are several factors to keep in mind. The foremost factor is the child's level of deficit. A child with a severe deficit would not be an appropriate candidate to be tutored. Likewise, a child whose behavior is difficult to manage would not make an appropriate candidate. Another factor to consider is the age of the tutee and tutor. It has been my experience that the farther apart the ages of the tutee and tutor, the better the pair work together. The older tutor often finds it more rewarding to work with a younger child. On the other hand, the older tutor is someone the younger tutee can look up to.

In my school, to be a tutor is an honor. Tutors are chosen by the classroom teachers. Criteria used for choosing tutors are responsibility, completion of assignments, good social skills, and average to above average achievement in reading. Some teachers use tutoring as a lever to increase the tutor's work rate. Tutoring becomes an incentive to complete all their assignments. *Marianne Abbey, Title I Teacher, Garden Hills School, Champaign, Illinois* work or sometimes work on their classroom assignments outside of school time so that they can qualify as tutors. Their classroom teachers may also perceive tutoring positively. Apart from the fact that tutoring is a worthwhile activity that will help the children grow in social maturity, the classroom teacher can take advantage of the students' desire to tutor and use it as a means of motivating them to keep up their assigned work. Moreover, during the period when the student tutors are gone from the classroom the teachers can capitalize on the reduced class size and concentrate their efforts on the less able students.

There is more to consider than age, grade, and ability levels, however. The crucial factors in tutor selection relate to the tutors' personal characteristics. Program organizers normally seek children who are dependable, responsible, sensitive, and caring, or children who appear likely to develop these characteristics. Classroom teachers are usually able to identify at least three to five children in their classes who possess these characteristics along with the requisite academic competence and sufficient time in their daily schedules to participate in a tutoring program.

In pairing tutors with learners, teachers need to decide about such factors as age differentials between members of the dyad along with racial and sexual composition of the pairs. Only sparse research data are available to help teachers with these decisions and none of these data would qualify as definitive. For example, while children prefer to be tutored by and to tutor same sex partners, and this is consistent with teachers' inclinations in matching tutors with students, there is no evidence to suggest that either cross sex or same sex pairings are more effective. The single study on this topic (Klentschy, 1972) found no relation between achievement gains and sex pairings.

With respect to the race of tutor and learner, our scientific information base is similarly vague. Witte (1972) found that various racial pairings had no discernible influence on learning, but that interracial dyads did positively influence cross racial interaction and acceptance. Other research has not found attitudinal change resulting from interracial pairings (McMonagle, 1972). Common sense, however, favors both interracial as well as cross socioeconomic class tutoring as a means of producing a positively structured contact between children of different backgrounds. The same common sense cautions against uniformly placing minority and lower SES children into the learner role while reserving tutor status to the middle class, white children. Children from all backgrounds can benefit from functioning in a human service, helping program. In addition to the interracial contacts within the tutoring dyads, a certain amount of camaraderie and esprit de corps can develop within the tutor group itself, thereby enhancing the relations among children from different economic and racial backgrounds who have come to share common interests, responsibilities, and problems associated with teaching.

Age pairings of tutors and learners have been investigated in two studies (Linton, 1973; Thomas, 1972). Both reported that older tutors were more effective than younger ones, but these findings should not be widely generalized. In one study, 12th graders produced larger math achievement gains than did 8th or 10th graders when tutoring 8th grade students. In the other, college students compared with 6th grade tutors produced larger vocabulary growth in second grade learners, but no differences were found in reading comprehension and oral reading measures. The dynamics of peer versus cross age pairings are not well understood. Intuitively, children might be expected to accept instruction from an older student more readily as this situation more closely approximates the classical adult-child instructional arrangement. In contrast, instruction from a peer might invite negative self evaluations with respect to status and competence. An age differential may also give the tutor an upper hand in matters of discipline. In contrast, teachers have organized highly effective within class tutoring programs that featured same age pairings. Lovitt and Fantasia (1980), for example, designed peer tutoring in a learning disabilities classroom in which these children helped each other acquire personal information data (e.g., name, address, phone number, etc.). On the laboratory side, Allen and Feldman (1975) found that compared to adults, children were better able to discriminate another person's level of understanding, using nonverbal cues alone.

4 Considerations in Implementing a Tutoring Program

The responsibility of providing every child with an appropriate instructional program belongs to the teacher. This fact does not change when teachers implement a cross age tutoring program. The teacher is still the person in charge. He or she establishes the instructional goals, delineates objectives, designs the lessons, chooses materials, and makes adjustments in instructional conditions as they are needed. By establishing a tutoring program, the teacher can intensify instructional services, providing more practice and individual attention to the children he or she serves, but he or she cannot justifiably turn over his or her professional responsibilities to the tutors. While a tutoring program requires that the teacher exchange some direct teaching duties for some managerial duties, the major instructional decisions (who to teach, what to teach, and how to teach) are still the teacher's. Below is a brief outline of some of the important decisions and activities for teachers who implement a cross age tutoring program.

DETERMINING WHICH CHILDREN CAN BE TUTORED

Not every child with learning problems can be taught effectively by a cross age tutor. Surprisingly, though, most children can, if the situation is properly structured. The exceptions tend to be students who pose serious behavior management problems, who are dangerously aggressive, or who are unusually noncompliant. If a child fits this description, he or she may not be "tutor material" unless an adult were to serve as tutor.

In beginning a tutoring program a good rule to follow is to start small. The teacher should identify four to six students who would

POSITIVE REGARD BETWEEN TUTOR AND LEARNER

Cross Age Tutors Can Be More Popular Than the Teacher

Scott, a fourth grade youngster 2½ years behind in reading, was being tutored by the special education resource room teacher. Due to scheduling problems he had to be tutored during his lunch recess two times a week. Scott was not terribly enthusiastic about missing lunch recess and his teacher had to "find" him on those days. Later, as part of a cross age tutoring program, Scott was assigned a fifth grade girl, Kelly. With Kelly as his tutor, Scott always came to the resource room voluntarily. Scott and Kelly formed a good relationship and both gave up more recess time to make a "sticker poster for good work" which was hung in the resource room. In fact, Scott enjoyed being tutored by Kelly more than by the teacher. His own involvement in planning his lesson, and his perception of Kelly's commitment toward his learning to read, made noon recess an acceptable sacrifice. *LMJ, Special Education Resource Teacher*

On Being Tutored by Another Youngster

My children like working with their tutors more than anything else! P.E., music, and other activities which are usually favorites with children don't have as much appeal for them as the one to one companionship with their tutors. *Mary Davis, 2nd Grade Teacher, Audubon School, Redmond, Washington*

Friendships from Tutoring

Some children work better with children than with adults. I have had tutors and tutees ask if they can come in during lunch to read so the tutee can catch up. Some children need that special friend and the attention that a tutor can provide. I have witnessed these friendships not only in my classroom, but in the halls, lunchroom, and playground. For some children, this special attention is very important in helping establish a positive self concept. *Mary Anne Abbey, Title I Teacher, Garden Hills School, Champaign, Illinois*

Kara, a sixth grader, tutored Michael, a third grader, in reading. Kara's parents reported that she commented daily on Michael and his reading lesson. "She talks about her job all the time." Michael must also talk about Kara, for at Christmas, Michael made "candy sundaes" for Kara and his resource room teacher. Expressions of caring such as these are not uncommon. *LMJ*

Sometimes Your Feelings Can Get Hurt

Mick, a youngster I tutored in reading, announced that he heard I was training tutors. I replied, yes, that was so. Mich asked if he could have Allen for his tutor. I asked him if he would rather have Allen than me. He said yes. *LMJ* seem to be good candidates for tutorial instruction, ones who need intensified services in the form of additional practice, but who do not have *serious* behavior management problems. The next step is to assess the students' mastery of curriculum objectives, identifying what they need to learn next. The teacher should begin instructing them himself or herself so that lesson content and teaching procedures are appropriately developed.

PREPARING THE SCHOOL FOR TUTORING

For the most part, teachers have enormous latitude within their own classrooms and with their own students. However, in establishing a cross age tutoring program, teachers begin tinkering with conditions outside of their own classrooms and may inadvertently disrupt the normal workings of the school. Children will mention the tutoring program to parents who will in turn raise questions with the school principal and the classroom teachers. To lay the groundwork for a tutoring program, the teacher will need to discuss the program with the building principal and with the upper grade teachers from whom he or she will request tutors. The teacher will need to present a rationale for establishing such a program, pointing out how it will benefit children who are experiencing learning problems and how it will provide an unusual opportunity for older children to gain social maturity by enacting a human service, helping role.

The building principal and the classroom teachers of the children who are to be tutored need assurance that the special education teacher will maintain responsibility for the instructional program and that the addition of tutors will enhance, not detract from, current services. The principal will want to see a proposal for informing parents and gaining their consent, and will want to know how problems will be dealt with. The classroom teachers of the potential tutors will need information on the kind of students who are potential tutors, the time commitment involved from the tutors, the nature of the services their students will provide, the content of training, the supervision the students will receive, and the opportunities they themselves will have for involvement in the program.

Regarding their involvement, the teachers will need assurance that the time devoted to tutoring will not detract from the tutors' classroom work, that tutoring is in fact contingent upon maintenance of high quality performance in the classroom, that scheduling of tutoring activities will be adjusted to complement the classroom schedule, that they will be kept regularly updated on the tutoring performance and social development of their students, and that they will have opportunities to observe their students and to renegotiate aspects of their students' involvement in the tutoring program. They will need to evaluate their students' potential for tutoring against such criteria as demonstrated academic success, patience, maturity, and suitability for a helping role, and recommend those who they believe would qualify.

49

TEACHERS' AND PRINCIPALS' VIEWS

Carryover to Classroom

Four students from my class participate as tutors in our school's program. It is exciting for me to see their enthusiasm for helping other people. The time they spend tutoring is a valuable experience not only academically but socially as well. The tutors return to my class with a renewed interest in learning that seems to motivate others in the room. This is an excellent opportunity for many types of students to offer something of themselves to others. The benefits run high on both sides. *Valerie Bennett, 6th Grade Teacher, Ben Franklin School, Kirkland, Washington*

A Principal's Evaluation

Our school's tutoring program has supported our goal of improving the Garden Hills students' self concept. The program enables students to value their self worth. It identifies ways in which students can contribute to the welfare of the students and the school. It fosters a care and concern for fellow students for the remainder of the school year. You witness the verbal and social exchange of these students on the playground and in the building whenever they meet one another.

The resource teacher always informs me when a "tutor of the week" has been chosen. I visit the classroom when the student is tutoring and congratulate him or her. This visit is followed by a letter of appreciation and thanks for the contribution to the students and our school. *Phyllis Wilken, Principal, Garden Hills School, Champaign, Illinois*

Tutors Must Maintain Classroom Work

This program is *not* a baby sitting job where the tutor simply occupies a chair and listens to another child read. The tutor becomes a trained observer/recorder who encourages and reinforces learning. In my class, the child who accepts the responsibility of tutoring knows that he or she is performing a skilled task with an obligation to help another child. The tutor is expected to fullfill his or her own class assignments and duties and knows that if these tasks are incomplete or done with less than expected accuracy, tutoring privileges will be suspended or terminated. *Nancy MacDonald, 4th Grade Teacher, Washington School, Champaign, Illinois*

Tutors in Abundance

Mrs. O'Dea, a fifth grade teacher at Garden Hills Elementary School, requested in March that *all* of her students be trained for tutoring. She liked the charting skills and math application available in tutor training. She also believed that tutoring taught the youngsters to be responsible. *LMJ, Special Education Resource Teacher*

> **Tutoring Results Seen in the Classroom**
>
> After a tutor program has become established, response from classroom teachers is very positive. Now several teachers will ask me at the beginning of the year how soon we can start tutoring. Two teachers have said their students show more progress in reading when they work with peer tutors than when they go out for special services. *Ellen Pina, Special Education Teacher, Robeson School, Champaign, Illinois*
>
> **Breaking the Routine**
>
> Last year, most of the children assigned to my program spent a great deal of time in my room. Therefore, I had to find different ways of stimulating them for short segments or risk losing their interest. I used cross age tutors for this purpose. The children had a break from my voice and my expectations. After a tutoring session, I could teach the child with renewed motivation, both for him and for me. *Jan Walker, Special Education Teacher, Oregon, Illinois*
>
> **Tutors' Skills Can Influence Classroom Teachers**
>
> A sixth grade teacher, Valerie Bennett asked me to show her how to set up the charts that the tutors had learned to use. She wanted to keep a record of her students' progress in multiplication facts and to motivate the youngsters to improve their rate and accuracy. *LMJ*

Occasionally, the tutors' teachers are reluctant to release their students from the classroom for tutoring. It does require additional planning and raises the potential for hassles from parents or administrators. One strategy that has proven successful in gaining teachers' cooperation is to demonstrate first that the special education services are indeed effective. This can be accomplished through working closely with an upper grade teacher of a problem learner by producing notable growth and by supplying the teacher with materials and procedures that he or she can use. Having received recognizable help from the special education teacher, the classroom teacher is then more inclined to return the favor so that others can enjoy the same benefits. Moreover, after one classroom teacher has participated in the tutoring program, observed its value, and suffered no ill effects other teachers will be more disposed to cooperate.

DETERMINING A TIME FOR TUTORING

As noted earlier, the research on tutoring suggests that sessions approximately one half hour in length are ideal and that daily sessions are preferred over less frequent arrangements. Since scheduling nearly always involves a minimum of two classrooms, the learners' and the tutors', it will challenge the organizational and arbitration skills of the program developer (see Figure 3 for a sample schedule). As a rule, classroom teachers generally prefer to establish a standard time each day when children will be out of the classroom. Of course, these guidelines are not cast in granite; depending on the specific circumstances within a school, they may need modification. The special education teacher will need to plan a schedule with the various classroom teachers. A sample schedule is shown below.

Time	Activities
8:15 - 8:40	(Wed) Tutor meeting
8:45 - 9:30	Resource teacher: Small group (2) and individual student work (reading/spelling)
	Math tutoring: One pair
9:30 - 10:00	Resource teacher: Individual student (reading)
	Spelling tutoring: One pair of peers
10:00 - 10:15	Resource teacher: Individual student (writing)
10:15 - 10:30	Resource teacher consults with teachers or tutors or assesses new referrals
10:30 - 11:00	Reading tutoring: 11 pairs
11:00 - 11:20	Resource teacher: Individual student (reading)
11:20 - 11:50	Resource teacher: Individual student (reading/math)
11:50 - 12:05	(M,W,F) Resource teacher: Individual student (writing)
	(T-Th) Consultation with teachers
12:05 - 12:30	Resource teacher travels to afternoon school
12:30 - 12:45	Lunch with tutors—discussion of projects
12:45 - 1:15	Reading tutoring: Four pairs
	Math tutoring: One pair
	Independent work: One student writing
1:00 - 3:00	(Wed) Adult volunteer (certified teacher) assess new referrals
1:00 - 2:30	(M-F) Adult volunteer performs clerical work, constructs instructional materials, writes comprehension questions and substitutes for absent tutors
1:15 - 1:50	(M-Th) Adult volunteer tutors a student: (reading/math)
	Resource teacher: Small group of five (math)
	These students spend a portion of this time in peer tutoring
1:50 - 2:10	Resource teacher: Small group of four (reading)
2:10 - 2:20	One student monitors completion of the "take home" assignment of small group and tutors kindergarten youngsters on color recognition
2:15 - 2:45	Resource teacher: Small group of four (reading)
2:30 - 2:45	Spelling tutoring: One pair of peers
2:45 - 3:15	Reading tutoring: Six pairs

FIGURE 3. Daily Schedule Showing Tutoring and Adult Volunteers in a Special Education Itinerant Resource Teacher Program (Two Schools).

On relatively rare occasions, a principal or teacher has refused to release tutors during classroom time. In this circumstance, the more persistent program developer may wish to explore the possibility of scheduling tutoring during lunch break, recess, or after school. While this option is clearly less desirable than incorporating tutoring within the regular school day, it is sometimes the only one available to a new program. Once established, tutoring programs usually draw favorable attention and strong endorsements from parents of tutors. This support, along with the children's enthusiasm for tutoring and the demonstrated learning resulting from the individual instruction, can be helpful in gaining acceptance for incorporating the program within the school day.

INFORMING PARENTS ABOUT THE PROGRAM

The parents of potential tutors will need to be informed of the program and the proposed involvement of their children. This can best be handled by a letter which states that their son or daughter, because of academic and personal qualifications, has been recommended by the classroom teacher for a tutoring position in which he or she will help another student. The letter should also describe some of the teaching and measurement skills which the tutors will acquire, the adult supervision involved, the requirement for maintaining high quality classroom work, and an agreement for regular reporting on the student's job performance. A sample letter is shown in Figure 4.

The building principal should approve the letter before it is sent and determine who (herself or the special education teacher) should answer inquiries about the program. The classroom teachers who recommended tutors should also have an opportunity to comment on the letter's contents. Once tutoring has begun, the program manager still maintains responsibility for keeping classroom teachers and parents informed about the performance of the tutors.

DESIGNING LESSONS AND A MEASUREMENT SYSTEM

Tutors are not skilled diagnosticians, curriculum developers, or experts in designing instruction. These are teacher competencies and responsibilities. The data on the effects of unstructured programs point out the dangers of delegating too many decisions to student tutors. Decisions about the content of instruction are among the first to be made by teachers. Research evidence and personal experience lead us to recommend that the content of tutoring lessons be closely aligned with the learner's regular classroom programs. For example, lessons can be structured that use the same reading and spelling curriculum that is used in the classroom. A typical beginning reading lesson conducted by a tutor would involve several minutes' work on letter sounds, several minutes' instruction on new words, with the remainder of the period devoted to oral reading. For an older student, the teacher might replace the letter sound and new word practice with word meaning instruction, error word drill following the oral reading, and answering comprehension questions. The basic structure of the lessons changes little from day to day, but the content, which follows the classroom reading series, is adjusted in accordance with the learner's demonstration of mastery. Thus, the tutors do not have to invent each day's lesson anew; rather, they follow an established lesson format.

The teacher needs to develop a procedure for measuring students' performance on each aspect of reading. The tutors can measure and chart progress daily as their students gain in competence, and the

---

Dear _____

Your son (daughter) has been recommended by _____ to be a student tutor at Audubon Elementary School. His teacher believes that _____ has demonstrated the academic success, patience, and maturity needed to help another youngster experience more academic success in school. In a cross age tutoring program, your son will be a model and a special teacher to a younger child.

The recommended youngsters at Audubon Elementary School will participate in a 2 week training program. They will be instructed in some basic techniques to teach reading. The tutors will also learn to use a stopwatch and a calculator to compute oral reading rate and percentage correct. In the tutoring program, a data based instructional program will be used and the tutors will learn to chart and interpret several kinds of graphs.

The training and management of the tutoring program will be under my constant supervision. A quarterly report of your child's tutoring experiences will be sent to you. It is also understood by the principal, classroom teacher, and me that _____ will maintain his high academic achievements and exemplary social behavior at school in order to continue in the tutoring program. If you have any questions please call me or come to see me at Audubon in the afternoon. Parents are invited to visit the tutoring program at any time.
Sincerely,

Linda Jenkins
Resource Room Teacher

Yes, _____ has my permission to participate in the tutoring program at Audubon.

_____
Parent's signature

FIGURE 4. A Sample Letter to Parents of Potential Tutors.

teacher can employ these data in making instructional modifications for particular students. For example, the teacher may note that a story needs to be repeated, that letter sounds are being introduced too slowly, that vocabulary needs to be overlearned for purposes of retention, or that a change in incentives may be required to motivate the student to work more diligently. Sample charts kept by tutors enable the teacher to monitor children's progress daily. Following is a suggested method for recording performance and progress for individual students.

Measuring Performance and Progress

A teacher can maintain three types of visual data displays (charts) for each child served. These include a daily performance chart, a daily progress (in the curriculum) chart, and an annual progress chart.

Daily Performance Chart

The daily performance chart can be used to monitor the student's functioning on those behaviors that are directly taught. For example, using the bands on Sterling's performance chart (see Figure 5) his reading accuracy (top band), oral reading rate (second band), letter sound accuracy (third band) and comprehension accuracy (fourth band) are monitored. The reading accuracy and rate data are based on a 100 word passage drawn from the story on which Sterling is working. If Sterling reads this sample with less than 95% accuracy, he must work on that story another day. The comprehension data are based on Sterling's answers to several questions covering the story's content. He must achieve at least 80% comprehension of each story. The chart also tells his tutor when to introduce additional letter sounds within a level or to remain on those he worked on the previous day.

Sterling's chart shows that on September 18 his reading accuracy on the first story in Level 8, Allyn and Bacon, was 96%, his oral rate was 45 words per minute, his letter sound accuracy (Level 6) was 100%, and his comprehension was 100%.

Daily Progress Chart

This second chart (see Figure 6) is tied closely to the daily performance chart. It reflects the students' rate of progress through the reading curriculum in terms of mastering stories (95% accuracy and 80% comprehension) within the reading levels. For example, it reveals that on September 18, Sterling mastered the first three stories in Level 8, Allyn and Bacon. The straight diagonal line on Sterling's chart reflects the progress goal for him for the semester—i.e., mastery of Level 8 through story 3 of Level II. If Sterling were to fall below this line, his teacher would need to modify his program, perhaps scheduling more tutoring or changing some aspect of the lesson. Moreover, by referring back to his daily performance chart, his teacher can determine if the difficulty was related to reading accuracy or comprehension.

The tutors maintain both the performance and progress charts for their students. They share these data with the teacher each day so that he or she can determine if and when a program change is needed.

Annual Progress Chart

Whereas the previous two charts are plotted daily, the Annual Progress Chart (see Figure 7) is intended to reflect month to month progress in the curriculum. Normal grade level progress through the curriculum is depicted up the left side. For example, in the Allyn and Bacon series, Levels 6 through 10 are taught in Grade 1, with the 9 stories of Level 6 taught in September (bottom left box on grid). In Grade 6, Level 19 (24 stories) is taught during the first semester and Level 20 (24 stories) is taught during the second semester.

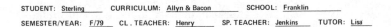

STUDENT: Sterling   CURRICULUM: Allyn & Bacon   SCHOOL: Franklin
SEMESTER/YEAR: F/79   CL. TEACHER: Henry   SP. TEACHER: Jenkins   TUTOR: Lisa

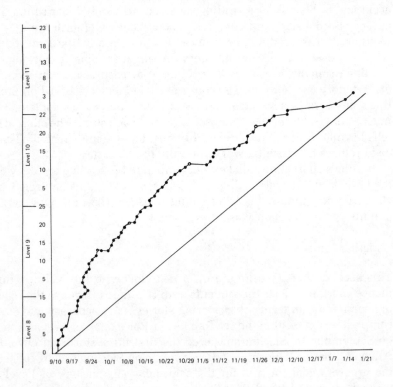

FIGURE 5. Daily Progress In Curriculum

56

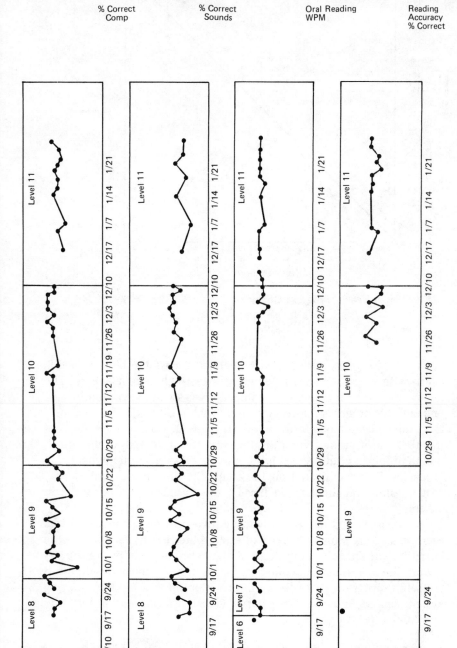

FIGURE 6. Daily Performance Chart

57

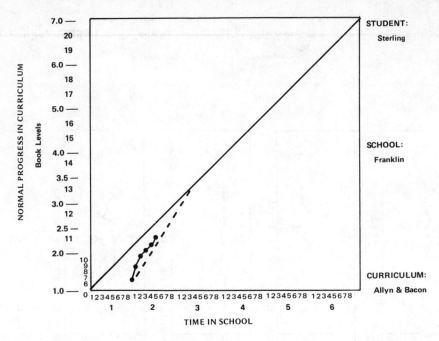

FIGURE 7. Yearly Progress Chart

The child's years in school are depicted across the bottom of this chart, with 9 months shown for each of the 6 elementary years. The heavy diagonal line shows normal progress in the curriculum—i.e., one month's progress for every month in school. The dashed line indicates the teacher's long term goal for Sterling. It extends from the first month of third grade (when Sterling was first referred) to the fourth month of fourth grade (when it is hoped that Sterling will be reading at grade level). As indicated on the chart, Sterling had mastered only reading skills taught through Level 7 during his first three years in school.

This chart is tied in closely with the two previous charts. It shows Sterling's actual plots at the end of each of the first five months of the current year. This chart can be used to determine a student's progress toward the long range goals that are stated in his or her individualized education program (IEP). More information on this kind of charting system can be found in *Data Based Program Modification* by Deno and Mirkin (1977).

Diagnostic Testing

In what appears to be an almost universal phenomenon, special and remedial education teachers or school psychologists routinely select and administer a battery of diagnostic tests to every child experiencing

58

learning problems. The avowed intent of this testing is to determine the children's strengths and weaknesses, thus enabling teachers to design an appropriate instructional program that will meet the special needs of each student. More specifically, this test information usually translates into decisions about what to teach and how to teach it.

We take an extreme position on the value of most diagnostic testing—that it is essentially bunk. Perhaps we should explain! For the most part, the tests and subtests within a "diagnostic battery" provide norm referenced information, either in terms of grade equivalent scores or percentile ranks, which essentially tells where a particular student stands in relation to other students. This information may be of interest in suggesting the extent to which a particular child deviates from his or her peers on a specific skill (e.g., sound blending) or within a general academic area (e.g., reading), but it is virtually useless for determining what to teach.

To illustrate, knowing that a child is in the 8th percentile of children his or her age in the ability to recognize words on the Peabody Individual Achievement Test does not help a teacher select for instruction the words that will maximize the child's progress in a particular curriculum. To do that, the teacher would need to determine the sequence of letter sound and word introduction within a curriculum, the curriculum's requirement for blending, and the child's mastery of those skills. Even criterion referenced tests, whether assessing word analysis, sound blending, or other skills, are entirely too general to be of much value for placement, if they are not correlated with specific curricula. The assessment needed for placing children in an instructional sequence and for designing lessons is neither arcane nor highly sophisticated. It is simply a matter of analyzing the skills taught in a curriculum and determining which of those skills the child has yet to master.

As for determining *how* to teach, no diagnostic tests or subtests are currently available that assess learner style so that teachers or psychologists can differentially match instructional procedures to take advantage of individual learner traits. Contrary to the claims found in methods textbooks, test manuals, and other authoritative sources, evidence to support matching instructional procedures to learner style simply does not exist. The most popular version of the learner style-instructional matching myth relates to assessing the learner's modality strengths and weaknesses. The idea is that while some children are primarily auditory learners, others are essentially visual learners, and that instructional effectiveness will be enhanced by matching auditory teaching methods with the former and visual methods with the latter. Usually, this strategy takes the form of giving systematic, synthetic phonics instruction (e.g., Distar Reading, a "predominantly auditory" approach) to children with auditory strengths, and whole word (e.g., Scott Foresman, a "predominately visual," sight word approach) to children with visual strengths.

To date there have been 14 studies that used a variety of modality assessment tools and a variety of reading methodologies to test this modality matching strategy with elementary aged children. None of these found that children who received instruction that matched their modality strength learned more than children whose instruction matched their modality weakness (Arter & Jenkins, 1979). These data should not be interpreted to mean that children do not differ on any traits that might interact with instructional procedures, for they most certainly do. For example, some children will work hard for a tutor's attention, others might be reinforced by earning an opportunity to play checkers, and still others may improve their performance so that they can earn the privilege of learning a magic trick. The point is that time consumed in pre-instructional diagnosis of learning style is not time well spent, at least with the current state of diagnostic technology. Teachers can provide their tutors with simple measurement strategies, such as the charts shown above, which will suffice to inform them when adjustments are needed in the instructional program.

DESIGNING AND CONDUCTING TUTOR TRAINING

The specific content of training programs to prepare children for tutoring will vary with the subject area in which they tutor, the kind of performance measures the program employs, and the types of children to be tutored. Nevertheless, training will usually address these general topics: information about the program and the tutors' responsibilities, measurement procedures, lesson structure, teaching procedures, and personal behaviors.

Program and Responsibilities

Trainees are given information on the purpose of the program and the responsibilities that come with being a tutor. Responsibilities pertaining to tutoring itself include the regular time commitment, punctuality, confidentiality, and positive regard for the learner. The tutor's own classroom responsibilities include maintaining the quality of work on their regular assignments and keeping informed about and making up any work they missed while out of the classroom.

Measurement

Since a program's success depends largely on the teacher's ability to make accurate instructional decisions, considerable training time is devoted to teaching the tutors the data system that provides teachers with the information needed in this decision making. Trainees learn what performance data they will collect (e.g., percent correct, rate of math facts, oral reading, and spelling) and the procedures for collecting these data (e.g., random samples of math facts from specified domains, preselected passages, and structured spelling lists). Trainees

ABOUT TRAINING

Additional Training

After a while, tutors will want to expand their teaching skills. Once my program is running smoothly, I usually schedule a training session on asking comprehension questions. My sixth graders have enjoyed learning the differences between literal and inferential questions. They even began analyzing the kinds of questions asked by their classroom teacher, and became so sophisticated in this regard that their teacher, Ms. Bennett, wondered if somehow she had been using these terms inadvertently while teaching. *LMJ, Special Education Resource Teacher*

Supervision

While the children are tutoring, I supervise by walking from pair to pair, observing and monitoring. In this way I can correct any mistakes that might be made. If the same mistakes are made consistently, then it is time to retrain the tutor. The retraining might be in a brief session after school or at recess, just on the deficit skills. If that doesn't remedy the errors, then the tutor is removed from the tutoring program and has to repeat the formal tutor training. *Marianne Abbey, Title I Teacher, Garden Hills School, Champaign, Illinois*

Tutors Can Contribute to Making Instructional Decisions

Lisa, an 11 year old tutor, had been taught the concepts of instructional and motivational interventions. Jerry, her 8 year old tutee, had always been cooperative, actually eager, to do his sound sheet and isolated word drill, and to orally read with Lisa every day. However, shortly after Jerry graduated to a new book, Lisa told me that he was complaining about doing his reading lesson. Jerry had been required to master new words introduced in a particular story. The number of words introduced in the new reader was now 20 to 25 as compared to the earlier average of 10. The first thing Jerry did when coming to his lesson was look at the number of new word cards and frown. Mastering these words before reading the story was aversive. Liza realized that the basic problem was the number of new words and that a new instructional intervention was necessary. *LMJ*

Charting

Charting is a very good learning experience. Most kids my age don't know anything about charting and might never know. It is also fun. It makes me feel like a real teacher. *Heather Jewett, 6th Grade Tutor, Franklin School* may need to learn how to use stopwatches and pocket calculators to compute summary statistics. In addition, they will need practice in transcribing performance data onto record sheets and charts, if visual data displays are used.

Lesson Structure and Teaching Procedures

Depending upon the tutors' academic specialization (e.g., reading or math), trainees learn how to teach specific skills (e.g., sound identification, sound blending, reading out loud, one to one correspondence, adding, subtracting), appropriate use of prompts, and error correction procedures. They also learn the various components of a lesson and the amount of time allocated to each component.

Training procedures for preparing tutors on these tasks extend beyond mere telling. Teachers can demonstrate an entire lesson while trainees observe the teacher as he or she models appropriate tutor-student interactions. Teachers can also model lesson components or small scale instructional episodes, and follow these with role playing opportunities for the trainees who exchange tutor and student roles with each other. Finally, tutors can be introduced to their jobs by allowing them to assume responsibility for parts of lessons, and—as they become comfortable—allowing them gradually to assume more responsibility.

Personal Behavior

In the category of interpersonal skills, trainees learn how to display positive verbal and nonverbal behavior, including active listening, conversing, and praising good effort. They learn not to show impatience, disgust, or disappointment. They learn that errors are merely a signal for more teaching, not punishment and disapproval (Armstrong, et al., 1979). They learn to approve and give attention to appropriate student behaviors and to ignore and redirect off task or escape behaviors. They learn not to interrupt classroom teachers while picking up or returning their students, and to avoid creating disturbances.

As we stated earlier, different tutoring programs will vary in their specific training content because they differ on important features such as their instructional focus and measurement procedures. Thus, it would be difficult to design and disseminate tutor training procedures and content for general consumption. The topics described here do, however, represent categories of information and skills that a program manager will likely address. Recognizing that application of a specific training program is somewhat limited, and would require modification and adaptation even for highly similar conditions, we have outlined in the Appendix how tutor training is conducted in one special education resource program that relies heavily on a cross age, helping model in providing individual instruction.

KEEPING TUTORS MOTIVATED

Do Student Tutors Get Bored?

When initiating a tutoring program, teachers and principals often ask me about elementary age youngsters becoming bored. "These are only 11 year old children!" In my experience, boredom is not a problem. Dropping out usually happens either during the training period or in the first weeks of tutoring. However, once involved in tutoring, most students develop a sense of pride about their accomplishments as teachers; this pride and social reinforcement from the tutee, resource teacher, and parents maintain interest and involvement. *LMJ, Special Education Resource Teacher*

Changing Pairs

Changing pairs can be important in maintaining children's interest in tutoring. Some tutors need and want "bigger" challenges. Doesn't this happen to us as teachers? We remember most the "hard core" special education child whom we helped to learn a difficult academic task. Other tutors enjoy teaching and being a part of the tutoring group but prefer the well behaved, easier to teach child whose lesson is "straightforward"—e.g., teaching addition combinations on flash cards. Both easy and difficult tasks need to be accomplished. A good tutor program manager must constantly assess both the needs of her students and of the tutors. A good pairing is one which produces learning for the student and satisfaction for the tutor. This aspect of program management is reminiscent of the school management situation where a principal suggests a grade change to a teacher in hopes of producing better teaching and a "happier" teacher. *LMJ*

Selecting a Tutor of the Week

Selecting a youngster every week for outstanding tutoring gives the resource room teacher opportunities to further reinforce the tutors and point out good teaching behaviors such as careful listening, outstanding praising, good record keeping, etc. This is also another way to augment training, because it reminds all tutors of the important aspects of good teaching and helps to shape and refine appropriate behaviors in some tutors who may have drifted somewhat from their earlier levels. Throughout the school year all tutors can be honored by this selection. *LMJ*

Continued on next page

The Tutoring Room is a Good Place to Be

The status of being a tutor is enhanced when the tutoring room is available before and after school and during recess. Tutors can meet here to have lunch, talk, do homework, construct tutoring materials, etc. Making the room available during the day also enables tutors to observe the resource teacher modeling good teaching behaviors during small group sessions (e.g., Distar) or one to one lessons. Seeing the resource teacher "tutoring" objectifies for the tutors the similarity between their role and that of the teacher. *LMJ*

Tutor Meetings

I had two meetings a month for the tutors. The first meeting was for discussion. If anyone had problems, we shared not only the problems but some possible solutions. We also reviewed specific skills, which always seemed to be necessary. The second meeting was a breakfast get together. I always brought orange juice and donuts, and we just had fun together. *Jan Walker, Special Education Teacher, Oregon, Illinois*

Tutoring: A Special Privilege

It is important to make tutoring a special privilege so that the tutors work hard to do a good job. I also provide incentives such as tutor luncheons and "Tutor of the Week Awards." Almost every day students stop me in the hall with the question, "Miss Abbey, can I be a tutor?" *Marianne Abbey, Title I Teacher, Garden Hills School, Champaign, Illinois*

Tutoring Provides Some Natural Reinforcers

I did not always write tutor report cards. They are probably not absolutely essential, but parents definitely appreciate the feedback. For example, Debbie Frank's mother requested that her daughter's tutoring report cards be included in Debbie's permanent record. Rachel Anderson's mother asked for a copy of her daughter's "report card" to show Rachel's grandmother and father. *LMJ*

Feedback from a Tutor

If the resource teacher didn't pay any attention to us I think I would make a lot of mistakes and I wouldn't like tutoring as well. I'd probably keep on tutoring even if we didn't receive a daily treat, but it is nice to have one. One of the most fun things we tutors do is to eat lunch together in the tutor room. *Jenny Sagara, 6th Grade Tutor, Franklin School*

Providing the Tutors with a Variety of Reinforcers

I have always used material reinforcers to help maintain the tutors participation and high level of commitment. My tutors can earn a daily treat such as peanuts, a pretzel stick, or a piece of candy or a sucker. On Fridays, if they have tutored every day, they can earn a package of gum, or another treat of equal value. The tutors are young people who are devoting a significant amount of their time and energy to this program, and I feel that adding tangible reinforcers can significantly help in maintaining this involvement. I always tell them that the tangible reinforcers they earn are analogous to my receiving a pay check and that, although I love teaching, I would probably not be as faithful to this work, if I were not paid.

In addition to the material reinforcers, I verbally thank the youngsters each day for their good tutoring, and I frequently write them a short note mentioning something special they did that day or that week. I also use a quarterly report card to inform the tutors and their parents about the skills the student tutors have learned as well as those they have taught to their student during the preceding quarter. In addition, I intermittently schedule a luncheon or breakfast meeting with the tutors. This is a good time to discuss any changes in procedures and to reinforce their tutoring performances again. Another reinforcer the tutors enjoy is the opportunity to use my room to do their schoolwork, make tutoring materials, or just talk.

Two other special reinforcers come to mind. A picture of the tutors group is easily produced and is a strong reinforcer. One year I had pictures taken of the tutors with their students. The principal had these pictures prominently displayed on the school bulletin board. Another special reinforcer I've used is an end of the year party for the tutors. The children bring most of the food, and I arrange the time and place, and provide opportunities to play baseball, volleyball, etc. In one school the principal felt the tutors had contributed so much to the school, he arranged for an all day field trip to White Sands National Park which was paid for by the school district.

In summary, I believe that it is crucial to devote some time, some money, and some thinking to help maintain the tutors' interest and enthusiasm. These youngsters are pretty special people who are performing an invaluable service. Their commitment warrants a commitment on the part of the "tutor teacher" to supply social and even material reinforcement. The benefits are worth the effort. When the school year ends, and I observe the long range effects of the tutoring program, on the children tutored and on the growth in responsibility and social maturity on the tutor's part, it is clear that the time and energy I've devoted to supporting the tutors is not only easily justified but provides a great deal of satisfaction. *LMJ*

BEGINNING TUTORING

By the time the tutors have completed their training regimen they are eager to get started with their students. As is the case in undertaking any new job, there are ample opportunities for mistakes even with the best of training. Thus, during the first few solo tutoring sessions, the teacher will need to monitor the lesson carefully and conduct post-tutoring debriefing sessions. For this reason, it is wise to stagger the beginning of tutoring with just a few pairs starting on a given day. As tutors grow more accustomed to their roles, monitoring and debriefing sessions can be reduced, but never completely dropped. The teacher can use the tutoring period to refine tutor skills, to observe and analyze learning and instructional problems for students whose progress is slow, and possibly to introduce new tutors into the program.

MAINTAINING TUTORS' INVOLVEMENT AND INTEREST

Like teaching, tutoring is not an easy job. It can try a person's patience, tolerance, and interpersonal skills. There are good days and bad days. But like teaching, tutoring produces many natural rewards for the instructor, the most significant of which is the change in skill and competence on the part of the learner. The progress charts that record the learner's growth over time help to amplify the products of the tutor's work. The charts and what they represent not only remind the tutors of their accomplishments and the internal satisfaction that accompanies them; they also provide recognition from the learner, the special education teacher, classroom teachers, and parents. Besides the satisfaction that comes with having helped another person, tutors are accorded respect and prestige from their students, peers, and adults for their enactment of the teacher role. This too serves as a strong reinforcer for maintaining their work.

Tutors need these and other reinforcers to persist in their jobs, since there are always competing contingencies which vie for their time. Keeping tutors motivated is a challenge to the program developer or special education teacher. Personal attention from the teacher — time spent with tutors in discussing the tutoring projects as well as other aspects of their school and personal lives — has considerable influence on tutors' interest and continued participation in the program. This is roughly analogous to the interchange and friendship that develop among teachers in the school lounge. Another means of maintaining tutors' motivation is by drawing attention to their accomplishments through quarterly reports; informal discussion with their parents, teachers, and principal; letters for their files or to their parents (see Figure 8); school or local newspaper articles; and comments and remarks that remind them of the importance of their contribution to the children they teach. A third means of maintaining motivation is through systematic scheduling of reinforcing events such as tutor luncheons, parties, awards, pictures, and meetings. This combination of reinforcers ranging from intrinsic to extrinsic motivators has proven successful in holding the interest and involvement of cross age tutors for as many as 3 consecutive years of service.

FIGURE 8. A Tutoring Report Card for Parents.

Dear Mr. and Mrs. D:

Theresa has done an outstanding job of tutoring Marie. Since November 26 Theresa has helped Marie to master and complete 25 stories in Level 12 and 8 stories in Level 13 of her reading series. She has also helped Marie master the individual letter sounds and sound combinations introduced in levels 9 through 11.

Theresa has become a conscientious data collector and proficient in recording this information on Marie's performance charts. It took Theresa 3 weeks into tutoring to acquire these skills, but she kept at it until she mastered them. Theresa has also learned to perform certain statistical calculations; she can calculate percentage correct for measures of reading accuracy and comprehension, as well as derive oral reading rate from a combination of time and percent data.

Since we began in November, Theresa has missed only one tutoring session, and that was because she had classroom work to complete. Indicative of her conscientious approach to this job, Theresa notified me of her schedule conflict and helped me arrange for a substitute tutor for the lesson. Theresa has devoted more time to tutoring than many of the youngsters in the room. She has come to my room on several mornings to prepare materials and to check on her charts. To help increase Marie's motivation to read, Theresa made a very clever sticker poster on which Marie earned a prize for cumulating good lessons.

I am especially pleased with Theresa's social maturity. She was the first tutor to volunteer to work with a youngster close to her own age. She is very sensitive to Marie's feelings and has done an outstanding job of helping her to feel positive about her reading progress. She has a special way of making Marie feel successful in her reading program and of involving Marie in her own learning. She has encouraged Marie to locate their reading books and folder and to set up the desks and materials for their reading lesson. This cooperation between the two is terrific. Her commitment to helping Marie learn to read is evident in the number of stories and sound sheets Marie has mastered. Theresa's kindness, sincerity, and responsibility are especially admirable in a 10 year old youngster.

Sincerely,
Linda Jenkins
Resource Teacher

5   Classroom Volunteers

In addition to cross age tutors, teachers can recruit other persons into school volunteer programs to help in classrooms. Parents were once just about the only volunteers found in schools. More recently, organizations such as the National School Volunteer Program (NSVP) have taken a more aggressive approach to helping local school districts organize large scale volunteer programs that attract individuals from a variety of stations in life. Some of the strategies that NSVP has used to recruit volunteers and structure their services are applicable to special education and remedial education programs. Drawing on the materials developed by NVSP we will present a brief overview of volunteer services, recruiting strategies, and procedures for managing volunteers in the classroom.

ROLES FOR VOLUNTEERS IN SPECIAL EDUCATION

Volunteers can serve both instructional and clerical support functions. Most volunteers want to work directly with children, but some prefer a noninstructional support role. Typifying the former services are direct teaching activities such as tutoring. Many of the statements made earlier about training, supervising, and structuring lessons for cross age tutors also apply to adult volunteers who serve as tutors. Depending upon the adults' experience in working with children, teachers may be able to assign them some hard to manage students, or some older students whom they would be reluctant to pair with student tutors.

Since they have other commitments, adults generally can volunteer only one or at best two days per week, thus creating a scheduling problem for teachers who wish to use them in a tutoring capacity. The

69

problem is that the children who would be tutored require more frequent, usually daily, services. With some ingenuity, however, it is possible to circumvent the scheduling difficulties posed by adult volunteers. For example, when teachers have access to several adult volunteers, they can sometimes arrange for each of them to come on different weekdays—for instance, in the afternoons—so that between them they provide regular services to several children. Such an arrangement requires well organized communication between the various adults so that they provide structured and coordinated services to the children they share. The responsibility for organizing a workable message and measurement system is the teacher's, but the benefits of additional services can far outweigh the costs of these management concerns. In an hour or two one adult can tutor between two and four children who without them might receive considerably fewer minutes of individual academic instruction.

In circumstances where teachers are not so fortunate as to have several adult volunteers and, thus, are prevented from arranging for shared tutoring, they can still obtain good instructional mileage from one or two adult volunteers. Teachers have trained an adult to assume their own instruction duties one or two periods each week, thereby releasing themselves to perform other needed services such as conferring with classroom teachers or parents, assessing new referrals, training cross age tutors, observing classroom behavior, or consulting with building staff on instructional or management problems. Alternatively, adult volunteers with special training or backgrounds in education have helped teachers in testing and assessment functions, a particularly useful service in preventing an accumulating backlog of referrals.

On the noninstructional side, adults can help with a number of support tasks such as composing practice sheets, flashcards, or comprehension questions; reproducing instructional materials; selecting and counting out reading passages for measurement purposes; tape recording text for nonreaders; and preparing reinforcing activities for children. Some caution is called for, however. If adults are assigned exclusively to noninstructional duties, they may not receive many of the natural reinforcements given to those who perform more direct human services. For example, they do not witness growth in children's skill, are not thanked by parents and teachers for helping their children, and generally are not accorded special treatment by either fellow service providers or the recipients of their service. Lacking these natural reinforcers, adults who provide noninstructional services will often need to receive frequent recognition from the teachers with whom they work, if they are to persist in their service role.

RECRUITING VOLUNTEERS

Several successful strategies have been invented for recruiting volunteers. Directly approaching community organizations about the need and opportunities for services—either by speaking to groups or contacting the organization's leadership—can yield a number of school helpers. NVSP recommends approaching such organizations as church groups, synagogues, the education committee of the Chamber of Commerce or Junior League, professional and business women's clubs, veterans' groups, garden clubs, senior citizen groups, retired teacher groups, as well as the parent-teacher association. Talks given to the organizations by volunteers themselves are particularly effective. Feature articles in weekly and community newspapers that describe a volunteer program usually can be counted upon to attract new applicants. Radio and television public service announcements can be broadcast without cost, yet attract substantial numbers of volunteers.

For example, a 1977 survey of senior citizen school volunteers in Houston revealed that 185 individuals were recruited as a result of group presentations, 51 by newspaper articles, and 27 by public service broadcasts. Posters in store windows, banks, and post offices have proven effective. For example, one half of Boston's school volunteers last year were attracted by posters appearing in transit cars and buses. Some programs have gained the cooperation of businesses and agencies to insert descriptions of volunteer programs in monthly billings and social security mailings. These larger scale recruiting efforts must be carefully organized and approved by school authorities, and often require the appointment of a part or full time coordinator of volunteer programs. Using some of the same strategies, individual teachers or small collections of teachers could, of course, take a more modest approach to recruiting a sufficient number of volunteers to satisfy their program needs.

WORKING WITH VOLUNTEERS

To maximize volunteers' effectiveness, teachers must acquaint them with the expectations of the school and their role in service provision. A general orientation is required to inform volunteers of standard school procedures and schedules such as signing in and out, holidays and special events (e.g., assemblies or field trips), notification of absence, emergency procedures, and policies covering parking, location of supplies, restrooms and lounges, and confidentiality with respect to students' records. Specific training focuses on teaching procedures, lesson structure, and measurement of student performance. A time and procedure for teacher-volunteer communication should be established. The teacher is also responsible for ensuring that volunteers receive appropriate recognition and frequent reinforcement for their contributions. In this connection, the NSVP recommends that teachers regularly tell their volunteers how much they are contributing to the children's development, prompt the children to show their appreciation, prompt other school staff to comment on the value of the services, report volunteer contributions in the school or district newsletter, and take the time to know the volunteer as a person. Additional information on establishing volunteer programs is available from the National School Volunteer Program, Inc., 300 North Washington Street, Alexandria, Virginia 22314.

6 Final Comments on Tutoring

The rationale for establishing tutoring programs is based on the assumption that regular education has many children who will fail to achieve at a rate sufficiently high for them to remain in the educational mainstream. Even within special education and remedial programs where greater performance discrepancies are tolerated, many children are achieving substantially below their potential and, unless something rather drastic happens, they will not acquire the minimum competencies they will need to function independently as adults.

If the educational system possessed unlimited resources, many more children would achieve academic competence than now do. But resources are not unlimited. Moreover, since teachers are responsible for providing instruction to a classroom of children, many of whom differ both in their previously acquired skills and in their ability to acquire new skills, and since the consequences to children for not achieving academic competence are both negative and lasting, teachers have little choice but to examine their own settings and use their creative energies to design nonstandard means for dealing effectively with individual differences. One nonstandard but apparently efficacious intervention strategy is systematic tutoring. In theory, a tutoring program enables teachers to increase the amount of academic engaged time for individual class members who require more instruction than is normally available under routine classroom arrangements. Again in theory, properly designed tutoring programs provide students with sufficient repetition and feedback for them to master every important skill in the curriculum without being pushed too rapidly and without impeding the progress of other students.

Most program evaluations have indicated that tutoring is an effective educational intervention and, by confirming that theoretical predic-

73

tion, have given indirect support to the explanatory concepts of academic engaged time and individualization. However, since most of the "research" on tutoring has been formulated as program evaluation rather than as theory testing or component analyses, it has not generated a great deal of information on the particular variables that differentiate effective from ineffective program designs. Therefore, inferences and prescriptive remarks about critical tutoring variables or program components must be considered as somewhat tentative, and viewed cautiously by practitioners.

Having stated these qualifiers, we attempted to summarize the research findings on several key issues that practitioners must face in structuring a tutoring program. With respect to instructional content, tutoring programs that attempt to complement and fortify classroom instruction (i.e., the child's regular reading, arithmetic, and spelling curricula) appear to have an advantage over programs that create their own instructional content independent of the child's classroom work. Further, tutoring programs that adhere to a mastery learning model, where children's advancement to subsequent instructional objectives is dictated by their demonstrated mastery of previous objectives, seem to produce stronger, more consistent effects than do activity centered programs that focus more on "teaching" than on learning and in which children are exposed to a large variety of instructional events.

To implement a mastery model teachers must design a data system that yields an index of child performance on instructional targets. Considerable evidence indicates that teachers who base their instructional decisions on regularly gathered child performance data produce superior achievement. Installing systematic data collection procedures is probably all the more important in tutoring programs because when tutors deliver instruction, teachers necessarily lose some of the more informal feedback they would ordinarily receive when they dispense instruction themselves. With regard to time, tutoring programs seem to be more effective when students receive daily instruction in lessons of moderate duration. Tutors who receive systematic training in basic teaching skills along with an opportunity to role play and refine these skills before service tend to exhibit more appropriate instructional behaviors during tutoring and to produce superior learning outcomes. In selecting individuals as tutors, characteristics such as race, sex, and age do not appear to systematically predict successful functioning.

Children in the upper elementary age range have proven remarkably capable of promoting learning as tutors and of eagerly assuming great responsibility. There is also a fair amount of evidence to indicate that children who enact teaching benefit in relation to their own cognitive, social, and personal development.

SCHOOLS' RECEPTIVITY TO TUTORING

Given the repeated demonstrations in the educational literature of the efficacy of this intervention, it is probably safe to conclude that adding a structured tutoring component to whatever now exists in a school's regular and special education programs will significantly augment their capability to promote achievement. So, where are all the tutoring programs? Were the proverbial visitor from another planet to tour regular and special education classrooms in a random sample of schools throughout the country, the chances are high that "it" would not stumble over a tutoring program. For all the demonstrations of successful tutoring programs and for all of the tutoring articles that regularly appear in practitioner oriented journals and magazines, structured tutoring programs are surprisingly rare.

It is interesting to speculate on the reasons for these conflicting facts—i.e., the proven utility of this intervention but its lack of acceptance. Several possible explanations come to mind. Teachers and administrators may not have heard that tutoring can add power to an instructional program. While some people may be unfamiliar with the data on tutoring effects, it would be hard to argue that almost everyone is in the dark, given the frequency of reports on this topic and the face validity of the idea. A different version of the unfamiliarity explanation is more plausible; that is, teachers may lack information on how to organize and structure a program, how to design lessons for tutor delivery, how to recruit and train tutors, and how to ensure quality control if they subtract themselves from the instructional equation. Some teachers are probably deterred from introducing a tutoring program because they feel inadequately prepared for such an undertaking. But lack of knowledge is, at most, only a partial explanation. On several occasions we know about, special education teachers were offered a menu of inservice training topics of which the "how to" of cross age tutoring was one entry they could select. Their interest in tutoring was not high relative to other offerings.

Another explanation relates to the anticipated cost-benefits of tutoring. Implementing a tutoring program will extract a significant cost in terms of additional planning, communication, and bother compared to keeping the current program in an unmodified form. Moreover, teachers may not be entirely convinced that for their particular situation tutoring will yield a discernible improvement and anticipated benefits of sufficient magnitude to justify the additional costs of a program change. If this interpretation is valid, then practitioners are in a sense estimating the reinforcement they will derive from establishing a tutoring program and concluding that they come up short. We believe that this explanation comes closer to accounting for teachers' and administrators' low receptivity to the concept of systematically designed, cross age tutoring.

It serves to explain why many schools are reluctant to initiate tutoring and why those that do tend not to maintain it. While it is hard to locate a school where tutoring is ongoing, it is also hard to find a school where tutoring has never occurred. Statements such as, "Oh, yeah, we had a tutoring program at Ben Rush School a couple of years ago," are commonly heard. The implication of these statement is obvious. The relevant practitioners either judged that the tutoring program "did not work" or that the additional effort demanded by the program was too great.

If well designed tutoring programs are indeed capable of producing significant help for children with learning problems, then it stands as a challenge to advocates of this intervention strategy to devise a way for schools to readjust the reinforcement value for program organizers and cooperating staff so that they are willing to initiate and maintain these programs. We have contemplated four general strategies that might be useful in this regard. One is to design a measurement system that will provide regular and accurate feedback to program managers (teachers) so that they can ensure that each tutored child is making satisfactory progress. Presumably, the observation and record of child change would serve to reinforce practitioners for continued involvement in a successful program.

The second strategy also involves measurement, but unlike the previous strategy it addresses summative rather than formative questions in evaluation. Program organizers might develop general measurement techniques and design data collection procedures that will enable them to estimate the magnitude of the tutoring effect—that is, the extent to which tutoring augments children's achievement over what would have occurred without this intervention. One potential design involves before-after assessments of children's progress in the school curriculum. Two indices would be computed for each child, one estimating the average monthly progress rate prior to tutoring (e.g., .2 months for each month in school) and the other estimating average monthly progress after the tutoring intervention (e.g., 1.0 month for each month in school). Another potential evaluation design is the classical experimental-control group comparison. If school programs cannot justify random assignment to these groups, then they might modify the design to include nontutored children from a similar school in the same district who would serve as a comparison group. The object of these evaluations is to determine whether or not the tutoring program is producing an achievement difference and the magnitude of this difference. If positive results are obtained, they should function as a reinforcer to the people who contributed to the program and should help maintain their continued participation.

A third strategy requires the involvement of school administrators. The idea is to begin focusing more attention on learner growth and to systematically and frequently reinforce teachers who assume responsibilities beyond the ordinary (such as managing a tutoring program) that result in problem learners' achievement levels that are also beyond the ordinary.

A fourth strategy is to provide budgetary and personnel support in the form of technical assistance for districtwide implementation of effective intervention procedures. Perhaps a teaching or supervisory position could be funded; the teacher or supervisor would coordinate tutoring programs and other data based intervention strategies. The coordinator would provide inservice training to special and remedial education teachers in how to implement and operate tutoring programs; help teachers recruit and train tutors; assist teachers in solving problems in program management; and develop a practical evaluation procedure that would facilitate decision making as to program modification. The primary goals of the coordinator would be to remove some of the obstacles that deter teachers from participating in tutoring programs, and to provide systematic reinforcement for program managers—in effect, to alter the cost-benefit data in favor of the benefits.

PLACING TUTORING IN PERSPECTIVE

The major advantage of tutoring programs is their ability to increase academic engaged time, and to provide more repetition and practice on important academic tasks. Of course, there are a number of factors besides academic engaged time and repetition that influence children's achievement. Consider for example, selecting skills with high transfer value, breaking tasks into learnable components, sequencing skills to facilitate acquisition, placing learners at appropriate points within an instructional sequence, programing reviews to enhance retention, designing teaching formats that allow for clear stimulus presentation, ensure learner attention and provide adequate response opportunities, and arranging consequences that induce high levels of motivation. If any of these are ignored, achievement will be negatively affected, whether the learner is in a general classroom or tutoring program. Whereas careful planning in regard to these items will pay dividends in any instructional setting, it is also true that the efficacy of educational programs can be considerably enhanced by ensuring that individual learners are given sufficient instructional minutes and adequate response opportunities for them to master essential academic skills. Tutoring programs are uniquely suited to these requirements.

Appendix

We present the following materials to illustrate, for teachers among our readers, how to prepare tutors for work with low performing children. This material describes procedures you can use to train cross age tutors for work in a special education resource program or a remedial education program such as Title I. The procedures were developed by Linda Jenkins, who is a special education resource teacher and, therefore, are most relevant for those of you who occupy similar positions. Of course, even similar programs differ to some degree so that procedures appropriate for one program may need modification in another. The procedures outlined here should be viewed from that perspective. They may be adopted, adapted, or modified to suit your needs in a variety of settings: regular or special classrooms and resource or remedial services.

OVERVIEW FOR TUTORS

Begin tutor training with a general meeting of potential tutors. Explain to the youngsters that their classroom teacher referred them because they are patient, understanding, and good students and thinks they will make good teachers.

Tell them they are the *first* kids to be so honored at their school. Remind them that they will have to keep up their own classroom work if they wish to be part of the special group. Describe the general duties and responsibilities that are expected of tutors. This would include the importance of using positive, nonpunitive teaching techniques, observing rules governing confidentiality, and making a regular time commitment. Also describe typical lesson contents and a general overview of the teaching and assessment skills they will learn but do not present so detailed an account that it intimidates the students and deters them from participating. Rather, the basic message is that tutoring is a serious, worthwhile and important job, but one that is also enjoyable and highly rewarding. Give them the parent permission letter (which their parents must sign) and encourage them to discuss this new responsibility with their family. Tutor training can begin when the signed letters are returned.

MEASUREMENT SKILLS

Trainees will need to learn about several aspects of measurement, including procedures for data collection and data recording, statistical calculations, and charting. These skills are taught in the reverse order of their use, beginning with charting. Introducing charting skills early in the training program enables trainees to practice them in subsequent sessions so that by the time they begin tutoring they have become quite proficient.

Charting

During the first tutor training session, teach the procedures for charting data on student performance and student progress. In our program, tutors learn to plot mastery of stories orally read on a daily *progress* chart. In addition, they learn to plot, on a daily *performance* chart, data on reading accuracy, oral reading rate, percent correct comprehension questions, and percent correct recognition of letter sounds. The charts on pages 56, 57, and 81 are examples of those that tutors learn to use.

Begin by describing the conventions for labeling parts of each chart. Give trainees practice sets of data and allow them to plot several days' worth of information. Construct "homework assignments" on charting and give these to the trainees until they are proficient. Be sure that trainees master the skills and, if need be, schedule special sessions for individual help. Some of the best tutors have had difficulty in learning the mechanics of measurement.

Computation and Recording Skills

Give trainees data record sheets (see the Sample Data Recording Sheet) and demonstrate where to place information on such performances as errors, tallies, percent correct, rate, and page completed. For example, give them hypothetical data on sounding, reading, and comprehension errors and have them tally these in the appropriate box.

Also give them hypothetical time data (minutes and seconds) for oral reading passages of different lengths (50 or 100 words). Teach them formulae for computing percent correct and oral reading rates (% correct x 60 sec ÷ total seconds) along with instructions on how to con-

NAME _____ BOOK _____

DATE	SOUNDS		ORAL READING		TIME			COMPRE-HENSION	LAST PAGE	OTHER
MO/D	ERRORS	% CORRECT	ERRORS	% CORRECT	MIN/SEC	TOTAL SEC	CORRECT W/P/M	+ = CORR. − = ERRORS % CORR.		

FIGURE 9. Sample Daily Recording Sheet.

vert minutes and seconds (e.g. 2' 35'') into total seconds (e.g., 155''). Fifth and sixth grade trainees easily learn to calculate percent correct, but at first lack an adequate conceptualization of its meaning. They also find it surprisingly difficult to convert larger units of time into seconds. To perform these calculations rapidly, especially those yielding rate data, they will need to learn how to read a stop watch and use a battery operated calculator. A good deal of practice is required before they become proficient. It is a good idea to reserve a few minutes for practicing these skills in each subsequent training session.

Data Collection

Training on data collection is best delayed until after the tutors have learned more about teaching techniques and lesson components. The following material describes elements of data collection that will be covered.

Describe how the trainees will test students' performance daily on each teaching task. For example, they must administer a brief test on sounds, oral reading, comprehension, and any other teaching task included in their lesson. In our program, sounds are tested from a 10 item sample drawn from a sound sheet; oral reading accuracy and rate are tested in preselected 50 or 100 word samples; and, comprehension is tested with questions at the end of each story.

TEACHING SKILLS: PRAISE AND REINFORCEMENT

Teach the importance of positive reinforcement—of praising and smiling—and the hazards of criticizing, frowning, and giving looks of disgust. If you have been carefully modeling positive reinforcement as the tutor trainer, you can call the trainees' attention to this fact and illustrate it with examples of statements you made earlier. Remind them how they felt when someone criticized them after they had tried their best, or how they would like to he told "Your charts are all wrong" versus "Your charting is neatly done. Let's plot some of these points together again."

Trainees are quick to understand the difference between punishment and positive reinforcement and enjoy discussing their own classroom experiences. Let them generate a variety of praise statements. Demonstrate for them specific praise—such as "good sounding out," "good remembering"—as opposed to general praise remarks, e.g., "good," "fine." Discuss the importance of honest praise—e.g., a statement that a student is "the best reader in the world" is not believable.

During the rest of tutor training, take every opportunity to openly praise the trainees. Point out your own verbal reinforcing statements after you've said them. Have the tutors "practice praising" when trying out skills with each other.

When my tutors have completed tutor training, the first question on their tutor test is: The *most* important skill a good tutor has is_____. Eighty percent of the tutors answer, "To praise well."

TEACHING SKILLS: CONTENT

Since most referrals are children with reading problems, we concentrate primarily on the basic skills needed for tutoring in beginning reading. Training in more sophisticated teaching procedures, such as those used for teaching word meanings and probing comprehension, is usually postponed until the students have experienced several weeks of actual tutoring.

Sounds and Blending

With respect to beginning reading instruction, tutors are given training on vowel sounds, digraphs, graphemic bases, and consonant blends as introduced in the school's reading curriculum. They are taught the basic teaching strategy of Model-Lead-Test derived from Distar and are shown how to apply it to the teaching of letter sounds. They should be given an opportunity to pair off and practice this procedure with each other. Next, tutors are shown how to use the materials they will use for letter sound instruction. In our program, we use a sound sheet with 10 sounds to a row so that computing percent correct will be easy for the tutor. After the training session on sounds, it is important to test each tutor on several rows of sounds the next day. Later, each student should be checked individually for knowledge of letter sounds.

The lesson on teaching sounds in isolation is followed by one devoted to teaching sound blending. Trainees are taught to apply the Model-Lead-Test procedure to sound blending instruction. They are also taught to coordinate pointing to letters with saying letters, to hold sounds, blend two sounds, and to "say it fast." The resource teacher should "teach" several words to the trainees, demonstrating good and bad models and leads, and pointing out when it is time to "test" the child. Again, the tutors should practice this in pairs. At this point, you will need to carefully monitor role playing sessions and shape appropriate teaching skills.

Error Detection

The next phase in training is devoted to the monitoring of oral reading and the detection of various types of reading errors. Teach the students about additions, omissions, substitutions, and teacher-helps or prompts. Provide everyone with a copy of a text and then orally read a passage to the tutors. First have them look for only one kind of error (e.g., omissions) and count the number they hear. In reading the passage, make some repetitions and self corrections, and discuss why these are not counted as errors. Next, introduce a second error category such as substitutions and repeat the exercise. After every error type has been introduced, read them a 100 word passage, making some errors from each category. At this point, they should count the errors, compute percent correct, and chart your oral reading accuracy. Continue giving practice trials until students meet criterion—i.e., their error count differs from yours by one or less.

Correcting Errors

Next, teach the tutors how to correct reading errors. For most errors, the correction procedure involves redirecting the students' attention to the problem word(s) and allowing them to try the word again. If they are still wrong, they are prompted to use a sounding strategy and if necessary are given a model. Sometimes the whole sentence needs to be reread. Point out how error correction during a lesson differs from that during testing samples.

Have the trainees tutor you individually in oral reading and in taking the daily oral reading test. Arrange for this to happen during tutor training time, during lunch, or possibly before or after school. If the tutor's performance is inadequate, reteach the necessary skills. It is best to develop good teaching habits before actual tutoring begins because the trainees are eager, and once tutoring has begun it is more difficult to correct serious problems.

THE LAST STAGES OF TRAINING

The Nature of Interventions

The last concept I teach during initial tutor training is the difference between motivational and instructional interventions. An intervention is said to be something we do to teach a skill. List all the instructional interventions they have learned in tutor training. Have them list instructional interventions they can think of which are used in the classrooms. Talk about motivational interventions in which students earn privileges or treats. Tutors are often interested in examining their own motivations for working hard in school and discussing the function of grades, teacher and parent approval, interesting subject matter, and self determined evaluative criteria.

We discuss learning problems and what kind of intervention should be considered, whether instructional or motivational or perhaps both. Viewing teaching this way reduces any tendency to blame the student with comments like "He is lazy" or "He doesn't try hard." It helps to foster the attitude that the problem resides in our instruction, not in the student, and that we are responsible for coming up with the effective interventions.

FIGURE 10. Sample Tutor Test.

1. The most important skill a good tutor has is:_____

2. What is the name of the chart that records mastery or nonmastery of a story? _____

3. What is the name of the chart that records accuracy in reading, sounds, and oral reading rate? _____

4. List the two kinds of interventions that can be used to improve a students performance. Can you give an example of each? _____

5. Write the formula used to compute oral reading rate.
   _____

6. How many total seconds are in the following:

   3 min and 47 sec _____ 2 min and 51 sec _____
   5 min and 22 sec _____ 1 min and 37 sec _____

7 Set up the appropriate chart to record the data given in this hand-out.
   (Student completes charts using sets of data)

8. Susie read a 50 word accuracy sample for her tutor. She made 3 mistakes in 52 seconds. What is her accuracy and oral reading rate?
   _____

9. List types of reading errors. _____
   _____

10. What are the three steps in teaching a child to sound blend a word?
    _____
    _____

11. Write 3 words that have a different sound for ea. _____
    Write 2 words with a different sound for ow. _____

12. BONUS. Joe read a 25 word sample. He made 1 mistake in 37 seconds. What is his percentage correct and his oral reading rate?___

13. What are the criteria for passing a story? _____

14. When giving a test on the sound sheet and the student pauses, how long do you wait before counting it as an error?_____

Testing the Tutors

It is important to have each trainee demonstrate proficiency on all aspects of measurement, charting, teaching content, and teaching procedures. This can be accomplished through structured role playing among tutoring pairs or with the teacher. In addition, I like to mark the close of formal training by giving a simple paper and pencil test that everyone must pass with 95 to 100% accuracy (see Sample Tutor Test). This helps to catch some misunderstandings and serves as a basis for discussion. Hold a conference with every tutor and go over any mistakes on the test. Later, write a note to the tutor congratulating him or her upon becoming a full fledged tutor. I usually include a little present such as a pencil with a special eraser and/or a small ruler. The tutors in my room have a designated place on a book shelf to keep their tutoring materials.

Practice Sessions

Although the students have officially become tutors, the next to the last step in training is to model a whole lesson with a "real" student. I have the tutors watch in groups of two or three. While teaching the student, I tell the tutors what I am doing. The lesson is somewhat abbreviated because of my running commentary for the tutors, but it enables the tutors to observe each lesson segment before trying it themselves. On occasion, I have had tutors teach only one part of a lesson and then I gradually introduce more components as they grow accustomed to their job.

Final Instructions

Finally, trainees learn the procedures for picking up and returning their students, notifying the resource teacher about absences, discussing their students' progress, and modifying their students' lesson.

PRACTICAL CONSIDERATIONS

There are several administrative hints which are helpful in initiating a tutor program. Have oral reading test samples counted and marked for each story in advance. Have stories clearly numbered. Have sound sheets made up for every reader that tutors will use. For the beginning reading books, produce sets of flashcards for new words introduced in each story and code these so that they are easily found and returned. Tutors should know where to find and return student folders, stopwatches, calculators, reading materials, and reinforcers such as stickers, etc.

These tutor training sessions take about two school weeks. It is apparent that many skills are not taught, such as asking literal comprehension questions, probing comprehension, correcting comprehension errors, teaching vocabulary meanings and teaching arithmetic operations. Nevertheless, training just described should enable a teacher to begin a small cross age reading tutoring program immediately. The tutors can practice what they know. It will take three to four weeks for them to be comfortable with their lessons. Special skills necessary for a particular lesson can be taught during subsequent training sessions.

References

Allen, V. L. (Ed.). *Children as teachers: Theory and research on tutoring.* New York: Academic Press, 1976.

Allen V., & Feldman, R. *Decoding of children's nonverbal responses.* Technical Report No. 365. Madison: Wisconsin Research and Development Center for Cognitive Learning, 1975.

Allen, V., & Feldman, R. Studies on the role of tutor. In V. Allen (Ed.), *Children as teachers: Theory and research on tutoring.* New York: Academic Press, 1976.

Angyle, M. Social skills theory. In V. Allen (Ed.), *Children as teachers: Theory and research on tutoring.* New York: Academic Press, 1976.

Armbruster, B. B., Stevens, R. J., & Rosenskine, B. *Analyzing content coverage and emphasis: A study of three curricula and two tests.* Technical Report No. 26. Urbana-Champaign: Center for the Study of Reading, University of Illinois, 1977.

Armstrong, S. B., Conlon, M. F., Pierson, P. M., & Stahlbrand, K. *The cost effectiveness of peer and cross-age tutoring.* Paper presented at the Annual Meeting of The Council for Exceptional Children, Dallas, Texas, 1979.

Arter, J.A., & Jenkins, J.R. Examining the benefits and prevalence of modality considerations in special education. *Journal of Special Education,* 1977, *11,* 281-298.

Arter, J. A., & Jenkins, J. R. Differential diagnosis-prescriptive teaching: A critical appraisal. *Review of Educational Research,* 1979, 49(4), 517-555.

Barnard, D. P., & DeGracie, J. Vocabulary analysis of new primary reading series. *The Reading Teacher,* 1976, 177-180.

Bausell, R. B., Moody, W. B., & Wazl, F. N. A factorial study of tutoring vs. classroom instruction. *American Educational Research Journal,* 1972, *9,* 592-597.

Becker, W. Teaching reading and language to the disadvantaged—What we have learned from field research. *Harvard Educational Review,* 1977, *47,* 518-543.

Becker, W. C., & Carnine, D. W. *Direct instruction—A behavior theory model for comprehensive educational intervention with the disadvantaged.* Paper presented at the 8th Symposium on Behavior Modification, Caracas, Venezuela, 1978.

Becker, W., & Englemann, S. The direct instruction model. In R. Rhine (Ed.), *Encouraging change in America's schools: A decade of experimentation.* New York: Academic Press, 1978.

Berliner, D. C., Fisher, C. W., Filby, N., & Marlieve, R. *Proposal for Phase III of beginning teacher evaluation study.* San Francisco: Far West Laboratory for Educational Research and Development, 1976.

Bohannon, R. *Direct and daily measurement procedures in the identification and treatment of reading problems.* Unpublished doctoral dissertation, University of Washington, 1975.

Carnine, D., & Silbert, J. *Direct instruction reading.* Columbus OH: Charles E. Merrill, 1979.

Cloward, R. Studies in tutoring. *Journal of Experimental Education, 1967, 36,* 14-25.

Cloward, R. D. Teenagers as tutors of low-achieving children: Impact on tutors and tutees. In V. Allen (Ed.), *Children as teachers: Theory and research on tutoring.* New York: Academic Press, 1976.

Coleman, J. S. *Youth: Translation to adulthood.* Chicago: University of Chicago Press, 1974.

Deno, S. L., & Mirkin, P. K. *Data-based program modification: A manual.* Reston VA: The Council for Exceptional Children, 1977.

Dineen, J. P., Clark, H. B., & Risley, T. R. Peer tutoring among elementary students: Educational benefits to the tutor. *Journal of Applied Behavior Analysis, 1977, 10,* 231-238.

Elder, L. A. The use of students as tutors in after school study centers. *Dissertation Abstract International, 1967, 28*(1-A), 74.

Ellson, D. G., Harris, P., & Barber, L. A. A field test of programed and directed tutoring. *Reading Research Quarterly, 1968, 3,* 307-367.

Feshbach, N. D. Teaching styles in young children: Implications for peer tutoring. In V. L. Allen (Ed.), *Children as teachers: Theory and research on tutoring.* New York: Academic Press, 1976.

Fink, W. T., & Sandall, S. R. *One-to-one and small group instruction.* Unpublished paper partly supported by BEH grant to the Center on Human Development, University of Oregon, Eugene, undated.

Foster, P. Attitudinal effects on 5th graders of tutoring younger children. *Dissertation Abstracts International, 1972, 33* (5-A), 2235.

Fredericks, H. D., Anderson, R. B., Baldwin, V. L., Grove, D., Moore, W. G., Moore, M., & Beaird, J. H. *The identification of competencies of teachers of the severely handicapped.* Unpublished manuscript, Teaching Research, Monmouth, Oregon, undated.

Frostig, M., & Horne, D. *The Frostig program for the development of visual perception: Teachers guide.* Chicago: Follett, 1964.

Gartner, A., Kohler, M., & Reissman, F. *Children teach children: Learning by teaching.* New York: Harper & Row, 1971.

Glass, G. V., & Smith, M. L. *Meta-analysis of research on the relationship of class-size and achievement.* Laboratory of Educational Research, University of Colorado, 1978.

Haggerty, M. The effects of being a tutor and being a counseler in a group on self concept and achievement of underachieving adolescent males. *Disser-*

90

tation Abstracts International, 1971, *31,* (9-A), 4460.

Haring, N. G., & Bateman, B. *Teaching the learning disabled child.* Englewood Cliffs NJ: Prentice-Hall, 1977.

Harrison, G. V. *The effects of trained and untrained student tutors on the criterion performance of disadvantaged first graders.* Paper presented at the meeting of the American Education Research Association, Los Angeles, March 1969.

Harrison, G. V. *The structured tutoring model.* Provo UT: Brigham Young University Press, 1971.

Harrision, G. V., & Brimley, V. *The use of structured tutoring techniques in teaching low achieving six year olds to read.* Paper presented at the annual meeting of the American Educational Research Association, New York City, February, 1971.

Haynes, M., Personal communication, 1977.

Jenkins, J. R., Mayhall, W. F., Peschka, C., & Jenkins, L. M. Comparing small group and tutorial instruction in resource rooms. *Exceptional Children,* 1974, *40,* 245-250.

Jenkins, J. R., Mayhall, W. F., Peschka, C., & Townsend, V. Using direct and daily measures to influence learning. *Journal of Learning Disabilities,* 1974, *7,* 14-17.

Jenkins, J. R., & Mayhall, W. F. Development and evaluation of a resource teacher program. Reprinted in E. L. Meyen (Ed.), *Basic readings in the study of exceptional children and youth,* 1979, *11*(10), 607, 617.

Jenkins, J. R., & Pany, D. Standardized achievement tests: How useful for special education? *Exceptional Children,* 1978, *44,* 448-453.

Jones, W. C. *Some effects of tutoring experiences on tutoring and tutored children.* Doctoral dissertation, University of Georgia, 1974. University Microfilms No. 74-04825.

Kelly, M. R. Pupil tutoring in reading of low achieving second grade pupils by low achieving fourth-grade pupils. *Dissertation Abstracts International,* 1972, *32*(9-A), 4881.

Kephart, N. C. *The slow learner in the classroom.* Columbus OH: Charles E. Merrill, 1960.

King, T. *Affective outcomes of cross-age tutoring.* Unpublished manuscript, 1979.

Klentschy, M. P. *An examination of sex-pairing effectiveness for reading tutoring.* Paper presented at annual meeting of the California Educational Research Association, San Diego, November 1971.

Klentschy, M. P. *The effect of sixth-grade tutors on the word attack attainment of second graders.* Paper presented at annual meeting of the California Educational Research Association, San Jose, November, 1972.

Klosterman, R. The effectiveness of a diagnostically structured reading program. *The Reading Teacher,* 1970, *24,* 159-162.

Linton, T., Jr. The effects of grade displacement between student tutors and students tutored. *Dissertation Abstracts International,* 1973, *33*(8-A), 4091.

Lippitt, P. Cross-age helpers. *National Educational Association Journal,* March, 1968, 24-26.

Lippitt, P., & Lippitt, R. *Cross-age helping program: Orientation, training and related materials.* Ann Arbor: University of Michigan, Center for Research on Utilization of Scientific Knowledge, Institute for Social Research, 1969.

Lovitt, T. C. *Managing inappropriate behaviors in the classroom.* Reston VA:

The Council for Exceptional Children, 1978.

Lovitt, T. C., & Fantasia, K. *Peer tutoring: An approach for teaching personal information to learning disabled youngsters.* Unpublished manuscript, Experimental Education Unit, University of Washington, 1980.

Mayhall, W. F. *Learning by tutors and tutees.* Unpublished manuscript, Crisis Center of Lea County, Hobbs, New Mexico, 1972.

Mayhall, W. F., & Jenkins, J. R. Scheduling daily or less-than-daily instruction: Implications for resource programs. *Journal of Learning Disabilities,* 1977, *10* (3), 159-163.

Mayhall, W. R., Jenkins, J. R., Chestnut, N., Rose, F., Schoorder, K., & Jordan, B. Supervision and site of instruction as factors in tutorial programs. *Exceptional Children,* 1975, *42,* 151-154.

McKenzie, H. Special education and consulting teachers. In Rev. Clark, D. R. Evans & L. A. Hamerlynck (Eds.), *Implementing behavioral programs for schools and clinics.* Champaign, IL: Research Press, 1972.

McMonagle, L. An investigation of attitude change in college tutors toward black children as a function of required tutoring. *Dissertation Abstracts International, 1972, 33*(4-A), 1521.

Melaragno, R. J. The tutorial community. In V. L. Allen (Ed.), *Children as teachers: Theory and research on tutoring.* New York: Academic Press, 1976.

Minskoff, E. H. Research on psycholinguistic training: Critique and guidelines. *Exceptional Children,* 1975, *42,* 136-144.

Mirkin, P. K. *A comparison of the effects of three formative evaluation strategies on reading performance.* Unpublished doctoral dissertation, University of Minnesota, 1978.

Mohan, M. *Peer tutoring as a technique for unmotivated, a research report.* Fredonia NY: Teacher Education Research Center, State University College, March 1972.

Moody, W. B., Bausell, R. B., & Jenkins, J. R. The effects of class size on the learning of mathematics: A parametric study. *Journal for Research in Mathematics Education,* 1973, *4,* 170-176.

Morgan, R. F., & Toy, T. B. Learning by teaching: A student-to-student compensatory tutoring program in a rural school system and its relevance to the educational cooperative. *Psychological Record,* 1970, *20,* 159-169.

Niedermeyer, F. C. Effects of training on the instructional behaviors of student tutors. *The Journal of Educational Research,* 1970, *64,* 119, 123.

Niedermeyer, F. C., & Ellis, P. A. Remedial reading instruction by trained pupil tutors. *Elementary School Journal,* 1971, *72,* 400-405.

Osguthorpe, R. T., & Harrison, G. V. Training parents in a personalized system of reading instruction. *Improving Human Performance Quarterly,* 1976, *5, 2,* 62-68.

Reynolds, M. C., & Birch, J. W. *Teaching exceptional children in all America's schools.* Reston VA: The Council of Exceptional Children, 1978.

Robertson, D. J. Intergrade tutoring: Children learn from children. In S. Sebesta and C. Wallen (Eds.), *Readings on teaching reading.* Chicago: Science Research Associates, 1972, 277-283.

Rosenshine, B. V., & Berliner, D. C. Academic engaged time. *British Journal of Teacher Education,* 1978, *4,* 3-16.

Shaver, J. P., & Nuhn, D. Underachievers in reading and writing respond to a tutoring program. *Clearing House,* 1968, *43,* 236-239.

Shaver, J. P., & Nuhn, D. The effectiveness of tutoring underachievers in reading and writing. *Journal of Educational Research,* 1971, 65, 107-112.

Smith, R. F. *Sounder: A complete reading tutoring system.* Bellevue WA: Edmark Associates, 1975.

Stallings, J. A., & Kaskowitz, D. *Follow-through classroom observation evaluation, 1972-3.* Stanford CA: Stanford Center for Research and Development in Teaching, 1974.

Stoddard, G. *The dual progress plan.* New York: Harper and Brothers, 1961.

Symula, J. F. The Fredonia migrant tutorial reading program. *Reading Improvement,* 1975, 12, 66-70.

Thomas, J. L. Are elementary tutors as effective as older tutors in promoting reading gains? *Dissertation Abstracts International,* 1972, 32(7-A), 3580.

Towson, S., & Allen, V. L. *The effects of evaluation of tutee on tutor's reaction to tutoring.* Unpublished manuscript, University of Wisconsin, 1970.

Werth, T. G. *An assessment of the reciprocal effect of high school senior low achievers in English classes.* Unpublished doctoral dissertation, Oregon State University, 1968.

Witte, P. H. The effects of group reward structure on interracial acceptance, peer tutoring and academic performance. *Dissertation Abstracts International,* 1972, 32(9-A), 5367.

Wylie, R. C. *The self concept (Rev. ed.). A review of methodological considerations and measuring instruments* (Vol. 1). Lincoln: University of Nebraska Press, 1974.

Yamamoto, J. Y., & Klentschy, M. *An examination of intergrade tutoring experience on attitudinal development of inner city children.* Paper presented at the annual meeting of the California Educational Research Association, San Jose, November 1972.